Best Of Friends

A COOKBOOK

written by

Dee Reiser   and   Teresa Dormer

"Sharing our best with you"

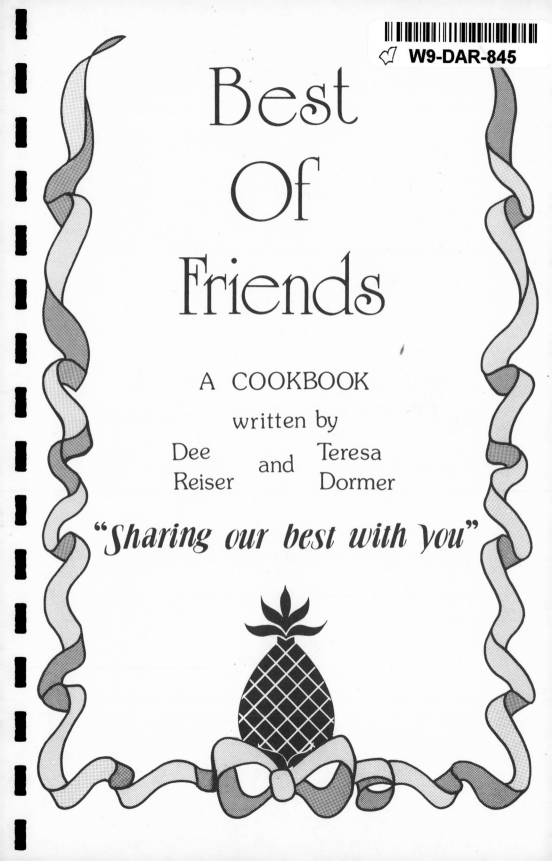

Library of Congress #85-090457
ISBN: 0-9615950-5-1

Artwork by Marshall P. Heintz.
Graphics by M. J. Davis

1st Printing—October, 1985
2nd Printing—May, 1986

Quotes scattered throughout this book are sayings picked up over the years and the original sources are unknown. We thank those people, whomever they may be.

Printed in the United States of America by
Wimmer Brothers, Inc.
5930 LBJ Freeway
Dallas, Texas 75240

PREFACE

We wanted this to be a very special cookbook. It began with our friendship and a shared love of cooking. As we talked about the cookbook, our families and friends offered their recipes as well as those from their families and friends. With the sharing of recipes, the circle of friendship grows and we hope it will continue to grow through you, our readers. Hopefully, you will want to prepare and share these recipes with those close to you.

"Best of Friends" is a fulfillment of both our dreams. Cooking is a way of expressing our love. Good food doesn't have to be over-whelming, it just needs a dash of creativity to make it unique both in aroma and taste.

Our recipes offer gourmet taste with a minimum of extra effort. Simply adding a few extra spices can turn a mundane meal into something extraordinary. We have created new recipes and revised old ones to present an attractive and delicious sampling of foods.

We hope that this cookbook will entice you to be creative and find the happiness that we have found in preparing and serving good food, no matter what style - simple or elegant.

Sharing "our best" with you,
Dee and Teresa

ACKNOWLEDGMENTS

There are several people that we would like to acknowledge for their help and encouragement and without whom this book would never have been a reality.

A special thanks to all our friends who so lovingly shared their favorite recipes with us. Their belief in us kept us going when the going got tough.

Pam Marshall, who provided all the artwork, is a very creative artist and a dear friend. The designs she created for us added just the right finishing touch. We appreciate the giving of her time and talent as well as her support of our endeavor.

The editing of our cookbook was done by another good friend, Susan Rush. Her efforts on our behalf are greatly appreciated.

Tom Crutcher is another friend who was always there offering encouragement and was a great help in editing the cookbook. Thank you, Uncle Tom!

Both of us would like to acknowledge and thank our parents. Dee's mom always allowed her the freedom to cook and experiment, and believed in everything she attempted. Teresa's parents, gourmet cooks themselves, gave her the confidence to experiment with different foods as well as the ability to combine spices and flavors to create just the right taste.

Most of all, we owe so much to our husbands and children. They continued to love and support us even when meals were late or when we were not at our best because things were not going well. Our husbands, Ed and Sam, really pushed us - sometimes harder than we wanted to be pushed. In the end, their belief and confidence in us was the cement that held it all together.

To each other ... Our special friendship allowed us the freedom to cook, laugh and cry together through the many highs and lows we encountered.

To all of you - Family and Friends - we show our appreciation by dedicating this cookbook to you.

Many thanks,
Dee & Teresa

ABOUT THE AUTHORS

We both live in Kingwood, Texas and met through our mutual love of tennis. Church activities, needlework, cooking and entertaining, taking care of our husbands and trying to keep up with our six children keeps our lives very active.

"Having grown up on gourmet food, cooking came quite naturally to me. My husband, Ed, and my sons, Doug and Jonathan, enjoy good food and are always willing to try my new creations. They are my best supporters and my worst critics. Their love and understanding is a constant encouragement to me."

Teresa

"Even though I began cooking as a small child, my culinary talents didn't blossom until I met Sam, who grew up on the spicy foods of New Orleans. Having grown up with the southern, home-style cooking of the Shreveport area, my talents were broadened by the combining of these two diverse styles of cooking. Our children, Sammy, Cindy, Sandra and Susan love good food from plain to gourmet, which makes cooking for them a pleasure.

Dee

Contents

Appetizers And Beverages

COLBY CHEESE BALL

16 oz cream cheese and
  chives (softened)
10 oz grated Colby cheese
1 pkg. Hidden Valley Ranch
  dressing (Original Recipe)
Pecans, chopped

Mix cheeses and dressing mix. Form into ball (1 large or 2 small) and roll in pecans. Serve with crackers.

Variation: Use plain cream cheese and Italian flavor dressing mix.

Everyone will want the recipe!

3-CHEESE BALL

1 (8 oz) package cream cheese
  (room temp.)
1 (5 oz) jar cheddar cheese
  spread (room temp.)
10 oz bleu cheese (room
  temp.)
1 small onion, grated
⅛ tsp. garlic powder
2 Tbsp. brandy
Ground pecans

Beat cheeses until fluffy. Add onion, garlic and brandy - mix well. Chill - shape into ball and roll in pecans. Chill again. Keeps several weeks. Serve with crackers.

TINY T'S CHEESE BALL

8 oz cream cheese
3-4 tsp. Heinz 57 Sauce
4-6 drops Tabasco
1 tsp. Pickapeppa Sauce
2 cloves garlic, minced
1 cup minced pecans
Parsley flakes
Paprika

Mix all ingredients, except parsley and paprika, and chill. Form into a ball. Roll in parsley flakes and paprika.
Will keep 2-3 weeks.

Everyone asks for this recipe; it's so easy, I hate to give it out!

The path to a friends house is never long.

VEGGIE DIP

1 small can chopped ripe
  olives
1 (4 oz) can chopped green
  chiles
1 large tomato, chopped very
  fine
1 bunch green onions, chopped
  very fine
⅔ cup vinegar
⅓ cup oil
Dash salt
½ tsp. pepper
1 Tbsp. sugar
½ tsp. garlic powder

Combine olives, chiles, tomato and green onions in a bowl. Mix together remaining ingredients and pour over vegetables. Refrigerate overnight and serve with taco chips.

SHRIMP DIP

1 (8 oz) pkg. cream cheese
1 (3 oz) pkg. cream cheese
1 Tbsp. lemon juice
2 Tbsp. Worcestershire sauce
2 Tbsp. mayonnaise
1 onion, chopped
½ tsp. garlic salt
⅛ tsp. cayenne
1 bottle chili sauce
★ 2-3 cups boiled shrimp,
  coarsely chopped

Mix together cream cheese, lemon juice, Worcestershire, mayonnaise, onion, garlic salt and cayenne. Mound onto a tray that has been lined with lettuce leaves. Pour the chili sauce over mixture. Sprinkle shrimp on top. Garnish with fresh parsley and lemon slices. Serve with crackers.

★ This is also good using 1 lb. of crabmeat in place of the shrimp.

Very colorful!

CUCUMBER DIP

8 oz cream cheese
2 Tbsp. mayonnaise
1 package Hidden Valley
  Ranch dressing
1 cucumber, peeled and minced
  fine
½ tsp. garlic salt
Dash cayenne
Buttermilk (for thinning)

Combine all ingredients with mixer and blend well. Thin with buttermilk to desired consistency. Great with fresh vegetables.

SPINACH DIP

1 pkg. frozen chopped spinach -
  thaw and pat dry
1 cup sour cream
1 cup Hellman's mayonnaise
1 pkg. Knorr's dry vegetable
  soup mix
4-5 green onions, finely
  chopped
1 can water chestnuts, finely
  chopped

Chop spinach fine. Mix all ingredients together. Store in the refrigerator. Better after it sets for a few hours.
This is good with crackers, breads or chips.

A hit with everone!

CLAM DIP

2 cans chopped clams
1 (8 oz) pkg. cream cheese,
  softened
4 Tbsp. mayonnaise
3 Tbsp. finely chopped green
  onions
4 Tbsp. chopped parsley
2 tsp. Worcestershire sauce
Tabasco (to taste)

Drain clams and combine with remaining ingredients, mixing well. Chill to blend flavors. Serve with crackers or chips.

Large fritos are really good with this dip. Great hit with the men!

DONNA'S DIP

1 (8 oz) pkg. cream cheese,
  softened
2 Tbsp. milk
1 (2½ oz) pkg. dried beef,
  finely chopped
2 Tbsp. minced onion
2 Tbsp. chopped green onions
½ tsp. black pepper
½ cup sour cream
¼ cup chopped pecans
2 Tbsp. chopped bell pepper

Blend cream cheese and milk. Stir in beef, onion, green onions, black pepper and bell pepper. Mix well. Stir in sour cream. Put in a small baking dish and sprinkle with pecans. Bake at 350° for 15 minutes.
Serve with crackers.

LAYERED MEXICAN DIP

3 (10 oz) cans bean dip
2 avocados
3 cans frozen guacamole
1 pt. sour cream
1 cup mayonnaise
1 pkg. Taco Seasoning mix
1 cup grated Monterey Jack
  cheese
1 cup grated cheddar cheese
1 cup chopped green onions
2 cups chopped tomatoes or
  halved cherry tomatoes

Layer in 12" round deep plate or platter as follows:
(1) 3 (10 oz) cans bean dip
(2) Guacamole (mix 2 avocados with 3 cans frozen guacamole)
(3) Mix together: sour cream, mayonnaise, and taco seasoning
(4) Cheeses
(5) Green onions and tomatoes
You may also add sliced olives, jalapenos or whatever else you like. Serve with Fritos, Doritos or Tostitos.

A very pretty dish!

A friend is someone who knows all about you
and loves you anyway.

JANIE'S "HOT" DIP
(Microwave)

3 cans Jalapeno pinto beans
  (drain and save liquid)
1 small onion, chopped
1 clove garlic
Salt, pepper to taste
½ moon shredded longhorn
  cheese
½ stick margarine
Jalapenos to taste

Place beans in processor, add onion, garlic, salt and pepper. Process. Place in microwave bowl and heat in microwave. Melt cheese and margarine together. Add to bean mixture; heat together. If mixture is too thick, add some of the bean liquid. Taste, adjust seasoning and add chopped jalapenos, if desired.
Some jalapeno beans are hotter than others so it's better to add chopped jalapenos last.

MARY'S CHEESE DIP

1 stick margarine
4 Tbsp. flour
2 cups milk
1 Tbsp. ketchup
1 tsp. red pepper
1 tsp. chili powder
1 tsp. paprika
1 tsp. tabasco
1 tsp. cumin seeds
¼ tsp. garlic powder
8 oz American cheese,
  grated

Melt margarine, add flour. Cook. Add milk and ketchup, then seasonings. Add cheese and stir until cheese is melted. Serve with chips. Don't let the pepper scare you off - try it - It's great!

Mary doesn't eat a lot of spicy foods, but she sure knows how to cook them. She surprises us at every meal.

HOT CRAB DIP

1 lb. fresh crabmeat
8 oz cream cheese
1 stick butter
1 onion, chopped
½ tsp. garlic salt
⅛ tsp. cayenne

Melt butter and cream cheese in top of double boiler. Add remaining ingredients and mix well. Serve in a chafing dish.
I prefer large fritos served with this; wheat thins are also good.

BARB'S CREOLE DIP

1 lb. lean ground beef
1 bunch green onions,
  chopped
½ green pepper, chopped
1 rib celery, chopped
2 Tbsp. margarine
2 lbs. Velveeta cheese
1 (4 oz) jar chopped pimentos
  with juice
4 tsp. chili powder or to taste
¼ tsp. garlic powder
Tabasco to taste
2 Tbsp. milk

Saute ground beef, onion, green pepper and celery in margarine. Melt cheese with milk in double-boiler or microwave. Add pimentos with juice and seasonings. Mix all ingredients together and serve warm with chips.

FRUIT DIP

1 (8 oz) pkg. softened cream
  cheese
1 (7 oz) jar marshmallow
  creme

Beat together and chill. Serve with fresh fruit. *Simple but Good!*

LIN'S FRUIT DIP
(Microwave)

1 egg, beaten
½ cup sugar
2 Tbsp. lemon juice
2 tsp. orange extract
1 tsp. vanilla extract
1 (8 oz) container frozen
  whipped topping

Combine first 3 ingredients. Microwave 1½-2 minutes on 70° power or until it bubbles. Stir and cook an additional 30 seconds on 70° power. Add orange and vanilla extracts. Cool to lukewarm. Mix in topping and refrigerate. Delicious!

Apples, pineapple and strawberries are especially good with this dip.

Friendship is to be purchased
only by friendship.

SHRIMP SPREAD

8 oz cream cheese
½ cup sour cream
½ cup chopped onion
½ cup chopped celery
Juice of 1 lemon
1 can shrimp, drained
Salt, pepper, garlic salt to
  taste
Dash Worcestershire sauce
Cayenne pepper

Combine all ingredients and chill. Sprinkle with cayenne when ready to serve.
Serve with crackers.

SHEILA'S SHRIMP BUTTER

2 cans shrimp, drained
1 (8 oz) pkg. cream cheese
⅛ tsp. garlic powder
2 Tbsp. lemon juice
4 Tbsp. mayonnaise
1 stick soft margarine
1 small onion, grated

Mash shrimp - mix with all ingredients - make sure it's well mixed. Chill. Serve with crackers. Can be made ahead of time.

SALAMI SNACKS

28 slices (⅛" thick) salami
1 (8 oz) pkg. cream cheese
¼ cup horseradish
¼ tsp. salt
⅛ tsp. pepper
2 Tbsp. sour cream

Mix cream cheese, horseradish, salt, pepper and sour cream. Spread thinly on salami (reserve 4 slices for top). Stack. Chill several hours. Slice in pie-shaped wedges (10-12 pieces each stack). Can be made a day ahead.
Makes 4 stacks.
Men love these so watch out ladies or you won't get any!

STUFFED MUSHROOMS

20 large mushrooms
½ stick butter
2 cloves garlic, minced
4 oz of crabmeat
1 Tbsp. minced parsley
1 Tbsp. minced green onions
1 egg, beaten
1 Tbsp. sherry
Salt, pepper, cayenne to taste
Bread crumbs
Butter

Wash and dry mushrooms. Remove stems and chop fine. Saute garlic and stems for 5 minutes in butter. Remove from heat; add seasonings, crabmeat, parsley, green onions, egg and sherry. Fill mushroom caps. Sprinkle with bread crumbs and dot with butter. Place on a greased cookie sheet. Bake at 400° for 3-5 minutes.

TORTILLA SNACKS

20 flour tortillas, (regular size)
8 oz cream cheese
4 oz sour cream
2 Tbsp. picante sauce
5 green onions, chopped
1½ Tbsp. lime juice
1 or 2 chopped jalapenos
½ tsp. garlic salt

Mix all ingredients together and spread on flour tortillas. Roll up and refrigerate overnight. Cut in 1" pieces to serve. Serve with extra picante sauce on the side.

Everyone's favorite!

CRAB PUFFS

1 can white crabmeat
1 jar Old English cheese
 spread
½ tsp. mayonnaise
1 stick margarine, softened
½ tsp. garlic salt
1 tsp. chopped green onion
Tabasco, cayenne to taste
6 English muffins, split

Mix together all ingredients (except muffins), adding the crabmeat last. Spread on the English muffin halves. Put in freezer 45 minutes. Take out and cut into 4ths or 8ths.
Bake at 450° for 10 minutes.

May put in freezer bags after cutting and pop in the oven when unexpected guests arrive.
May also serve them whole with soup.

ASPARAGUS APPETIZERS

8 oz cream cheese
4 oz bleu cheese
Whole wheat bread, thinly
 sliced
1 can whole asparagus spears
2 Tbsp. melted butter

Mix cheeses together with a little milk to spreading consistency. Remove crusts from bread and roll out thin. Spread cheese mixture on bread, add an asparagus spear and roll up. Brush with melted butter and slice in thirds.
Bake at 350° until lightly browned.
May freeze before baking, if desired.

SPICY CHEESE PUFFS

1 stick butter, softened
1 cup flour
1 glass jar of sharp cheese
1 tsp. Worcestershire sauce
⅛ tsp. cayenne

Blend all ingredients well. Shape into balls the size of olives. Chill. Bake at 450° for 8-10 minutes. (Can be frozen prior to baking.)
Makes 50.

Delicious and addictive!

CRAB CANAPES

1 stick butter
1 small bunch green onions,
 chopped
½ lb. swiss cheese
2 Tbsp. flour
½ cup chopped parsley
1 pt. half and half
Cayenne, salt to taste
1 Tbsp. sherry
1 lb. crabmeat
1 loaf thin sliced white bread

Melt butter, add green onions and parsley. Add flour, then swiss cheese and cook on medium-low. Add half and half, sherry, seasonings and crabmeat. Cut crust from bread and then cut into 4 pieces. Spread crab mixture on bread. Bake at 350° for 10 minutes or until bread is browned.
(May be made ahead and frozen, then bake.)

BOTY'S CHEESE SQUARES

1 loaf Pepperidge Farms
 regular sandwich bread
½ lb. shredded sharp cheddar
 cheese
1 small onion, finely chopped
1 pkg. slivered almonds
1 cup Hellman's mayonnaise
2 tsp. Worcestershire sauce
½ tsp. lemon-pepper
½ tsp. seasoned salt

Trim crusts from bread. Cut in fourths. Combine other ingredients and mix well. Spread about 1 teaspoon filling on each square. Freeze on cookie sheets. When frozen, put in plastic bags and keep in freezer. To heat, place on cookie sheet and bake at 400° for 8-10 minutes.

STEPHIE'S ARTICHOKE SQUARES

1 (14 oz) can artichoke hearts-
 quartered
½ cup bottled Italian dressing
⅛ tsp. garlic powder
4 eggs
1 small onion, chopped
¼ cup bread crumbs
¼ tsp. salt
¼ tsp. pepper
½ tsp. oregano
2 Tbsp. parsley flakes
½ lb. sharp cheddar cheese,
 grated

Rinse and drain artichokes. Marinate in dressing overnight. Drain and save marinade. Chop artichokes, coarsely. Saute onion and garlic in marinade until limp. Beat eggs in mixing bowl and add bread crumbs, seasonings, onion mixture, cheese and artichokes. Pour into well-greased 2 qt. (7½x11) casserole and bake at 325° for 30-35 minutes. Cool in pan.
Cut into squares. Approx. 40 squares.
Note: Can be made ahead and reheated at 325° for 10 minutes.

Stephanie is a very vivacious little lady who does all things well, whether it's playing tennis, teaching piano or cooking up delectable treats such as these artichoke squares.

The only way to have a friend
is to be one.

MINIATURE MUSHROOM TARTS

Crust:
24 slices thin, wheat bread
2 Tbsp. soft butter

Filling:
½ lb. finely chopped, fresh
  mushrooms
4 Tbsp. butter
3 Tbsp. minced green onions
2 Tbsp. flour
1 cup half and half
½ tsp. lemon juice
½ tsp. salt
¼ tsp. pepper
Cayenne to taste

Topping:
2 Tbsp. parmesan cheese
2 tsp. chopped parsley
Butter

Crust:
Use a biscuit cutter to cut center from each slice of bread. Brush muffin cups (use miniature muffin tins) with soft butter. Carefully press a bread round into each cup to fit. Bake at 400° for 10 minutes. Cool. May freeze, if desired.

Filling:
Melt butter, saute onions and then mushrooms. Simmer, uncovered, until liquid is evaporated, about 10-12 minutes. Remove from heat, sprinkle with flour and blend well. Pour in half and half and return to heat. Bring to a boil, stirring constantly. Cook a minute or so. Remove from heat, add lemon juice, salt, pepper and cayenne. Cool. Refrigerate or freeze in frozen bread cups until ready to use. Remove from tins after freezing and put in freezer bags.

Topping:
10 minutes before serving, mound filling into shells. Sprinkle with parmesan cheese and parsley. Dot with butter. Bake at 350° for 10 minutes.

ITALIAN CHEESE BREAD

1 loaf french bread, sliced in
  half (lengthwise)
2 cups mozzarella cheese,
  grated
½ cup mayonnaise
½ cup soft margarine
6 green onions, chopped
1 cup sliced ripe olives
1 tsp. garlic powder
½ tsp. cayenne

In a bowl, blend mayonnaise and margarine together, then add remaining ingredients. Spread on bread, piling up. Bake at 350° for 15-20 minutes until bubbly.
May freeze before baking.

A great addition with soup!

REUBEN BREAD

3¼ cups flour
1 Tbsp. sugar
1 tsp. salt
1 pkg. dry yeast
1 cup hot water
1 Tbsp. soft margarine
¼ cup mayonnaise
1½ tsp. ketchup
½ tsp. pickle relish
6 oz thinly sliced corned
  beef
¼ lb. sliced baby swiss cheese
1 (8 oz) can sauerkraut,
  drained
1 egg white, beaten
1½ tsp. caraway seeds

In a large bowl, mix 2¼ cups flour, sugar, salt and yeast. Stir in hot water and margarine. Mix in only enough remaining flour to make a soft dough. On floured surface, knead 4 minutes. On greased baking sheet, roll dough to 14x10 inches. Mix together mayonnaise, ketchup and pickle relish and spread down center third of dough length. Top with layers of beef, cheese and sauerkraut*. Cut 1 inch wide strips along sides of filling out to dough edges. Alternating sides, fold strips at an angle across filling. Cover dough, place baking sheet over a large, shallow pan half filled with boiling water for 15 minutes. Brush with egg white and sprinkle 1 teaspoon caraway seeds on top. Bake at 400° for 25 minutes. Cool slightly and serve warm. Cut in slices.

*Add ½ teaspoon of the caraway seeds to sauerkraut.

MARY ELLEN'S DELICIOUS HOT BREAD

Bridgeford frozen bread (3
  loaves)
2 lbs. bulk hot sausage
3 bunches green onions
2 pkgs. sliced pepperoni
Salad olives (small jar)
1 lb. grated sharp cheddar
  cheese
Tabasco

Put loaves in refrigerator overnight. Cut each loaf in half and roll out. Brown sausage and drain. Chop green onions and olives. On each ½ loaf rolled out, layer sausage, onions, olives, pepperoni and cheese. Sprinkle with a few drops of Tabasco if desired. Roll up and seal edges. Bake at 350° for about 35 minutes or until brown. Cool. At this point, you may eat it or freeze it. If frozen, remove from freezer (do not thaw) and bake at 350° for 45-50 minutes. Slice in 1" slices. Makes 6 loaves.

This recipe comes from my sister-in-law, Mary Ellen, who is a great cook as well as a great person.

MONYA'S MARINATED SHRIMP

2-4 lbs. shrimp (boiled and
  peeled)
2 large onions, sliced
8 bay leaves
½ cup tarragon vinegar
¼ cup lemon juice
1 tsp. salt
1 cup chopped celery
1 cup olive oil (Bertolli is best)
Few sprinkles of cayenne
4 drops of Worcestershire
  sauce

Layer shrimp, onions and bay leaves in dish. Beat remaining ingredients with a wire whisk until white and thick. Pour over shrimp. Cover and chill 24 hours.

OYSTERS CARIBBEAN

1 stick butter
6 chopped green onions
1 qt. oysters, drained
½ cup beef broth
2 tsp. chopped parsley
2 tsp. Worcestershire sauce
½ tsp. garlic powder

Sauce:
1 stick butter
½ cup flour
1½ cups milk
¾ tsp. salt
½ tsp. black pepper
¼ tsp. cayenne

Saute green onions in butter. Brown oysters in a heavy iron skillet until they form a crust on each side - add to green onions. Saute slowly 5 minutes, then add other ingredients, including sauce. Simmer 5 minutes and serve in individual ramekins.

Sauce:
Melt butter; stir in flour, blending well. Gradually stir in milk; add seasonings, stirring constantly, until thickened.

Delicious!

KATIE'S INSTANT TEA MIX

1 (32 oz) jar Nestea (lemon and sugar) mix
1 oz pure Nestea
1 large can Wyler lemonade mix
1 large jar Tang

Mix all ingredients thoroughly! Put in jars to keep. Use 1 scoop (from lemonade) per glass. Place in glass, add water and ice.

Great summer drink!

INSTANT CHOCOLATE MIX

1 (2 lb.) box Nestles
1 lb. box powdered sugar
11 oz jar powdered non-dairy creamer
1 (8 qt.) box powdered milk

Mix together and sift. Store in jars. To serve, fill cup ½ full of mix and finish filling with hot water. Makes about a gallon of mix (50 servings).

Kids love this! Great for camping trips, also.

HOT SPICED WASSAIL

2 qts. cider
2 cups orange juice
1 cup lemon juice
Juice from 2 #2 cans pineapple juice
1 stick cinnamon
1 tsp. whole cloves
Honey to taste

Combine ingredients and bring to a boil, simmer 15-20 minutes. Strain and serve hot. Makes about ½ gallon. Can also add rum, if preferred - for a festive touch.

My kids love a cup of wassail in the winter when they come home from school. Keeps a good while in the refrigerator. Pour a cup at a time - heat in microwave.

PAM'S POTENT PUNCH

1 qt. Hawaiian Punch
1 large can unsweetened pineapple juice
1 pkg. unsweetened Strawberry
  Kool-Aid
6 oz can frozen pink lemonade
1 pt. Crystal Clear
  (Grain Alcohol)
Orange and lemon slices
1 pt. frozen strawberries

Combine all ingredients in a punch bowl. Stir well and hold on!

PEACH FUZZIES

1 (6 oz) can pink lemonade,
  frozen
6 oz vodka or rum
2 Tbsp. peach brandy
½ cup chopped peaches, fresh
  if in season
Ice

Combine all ingredients in blender and blend on high until smooth.

A summer hit!
Pam and Gale taught us to make these with those wonderful Ruston peaches. Since then, our friendship has steadily grown.

PINA COLADA SLUSH

12 oz vodka
1 large can pineapple juice
1 (12 oz) can frozen
  lemonade
1 bottle Pina Colada mix
Cream soda

Combine vodka, pineapple juice, lemonade and Pina Colada mix. Put in covered container and freeze. Fill a glass half full with frozen mixture and half cream soda. Add ice and stir.

CACTUS JUICE

1 cup pineapple juice
1 cup vodka
2 Tbsp. confectioner's sugar
½ pt. whipping cream
Green food coloring
Cream soda

Combine pineapple juice, vodka, sugar and whipping cream. May add a drop or two of green food coloring. Shake well. Pour one jigger of mixture into a glass with ice and fill with cream soda.

A great drink for ladies or as an after dinner drink.

CHAMPAGNE PUNCH I

1 bottle chilled champagne
8 cups chilled ginger ale
4 cups chilled orange juice
1 qt. cranberry juice cocktail
Ice mold
Orange slices
Strawberries

Pour all ingredients over ice ring in punch bowl. Float orange slices and strawberries on top. Serve immediately.

CHAMPAGNE PUNCH II

4 bottles cheap champagne
2 bottles ginger ale
1 bottle Christian Brothers
 brandy

Chill bottles ahead of time. Mix right before serving and pour into punch bowl. Float ice ring in bowl.

This goes down easy but has quite a kick!

RED ROOSTER

1 qt. cranberry juice cocktail
1 (12 oz) can frozen orange
  juice
1 qt. vodka
3 juice cans of water

Combine all ingredients and freeze in covered container. Spoon into a glass. Mixture will be slushy.

FROZEN MARGARITAS

6 oz can frozen limeade
6 oz tequila
2-3 oz triple sec
Ice

In blender, combine limeade, tequila and triple sec. Fill with ice and blend on high until smooth. Run lime juice around rim of glasses and dip in salt, if desired.

PINEAPPLE DAIQUIRIS

1 (6 oz) can frozen limeade
1 small can crushed pineapple
  with juice
1 limeade can of rum
2 tsp. sugar
Ice cubes

Put all ingredients in blender. Fill with ice cubes and blend on high speed. If too thick, add a little water.

Very refreshing.

VODKA PUNCH

1 qt. cranberry juice cocktail
1 qt. orange juice
1 qt. pink lemonade
1 qt. vodka
1 qt. ginger ale
Ice ring

Mix all ingredients and pour over ice ring in punch bowl.

BRANDY SLUSH

6 oz lemonade concentrate
12 oz orange juice concentrate
1 cup strong tea
1 cup sugar
5 cups water
2 cups Brandy (added after
 cooking)
7-Up or ginger ale

Cook lemonade, orange juice, tea, sugar and water until dissolved. Add Brandy and freeze. Scoop into glasses and add 7-Up or ginger ale.

SPIKED WASSAIL

4 Tbsp. lemon juice
1 can (6 oz) frozen orange
 juice
1 gallon cider
1 tsp. ground cloves
1 tsp. crystallized ginger
1½ cups sugar
3 cups water
4 cups strong tea
1 qt. vodka

Make sugar syrup (sugar and water) and add spices. Let stand overnight. Add juices, simmer until hot. Add vodka. Serve hot.

A friend is a person with whom
you dare to be yourself.

Bread

LORETA'S YEAST BISCUITS

1 Tbsp. sugar
2 Tbsp. warm water
1 pkg. dry yeast
2 cups flour
1 tsp. baking powder
1 tsp. salt
2 Tbsp. shortening
⅔ cup buttermilk

In a small bowl, mix sugar with warm water, add yeast and stir to dissolve. In large bowl, sift or mix flour with baking powder and salt. Cut in shortening to fine crumb stage. Add buttermilk and yeast mixture. Mix to a fairly stiff dough. Knead lightly a few seconds on a floured board. Roll to ½" thickness. Cut with cutter and put in a greased pan. Let rise in warm place until doubled. Bake at 425° for 10-15 minutes. (If set in a warm oven, will rise in about 30 minutes).

Well worth the effort!

FINGER ROLLS

3 beaten eggs
1 tsp. salt
½ cup sugar
1 cup warm water
1 pkg. yeast
½ cup melted butter
4½ cups flour

Dissolve yeast in warm water. Mix all ingredients except flour. Beat in flour. Let rise 4 hours, then put in a well covered bowl in the refrigerator over night. Take out ¼ of the dough and roll in a pie shape. Cut 10-12 wedges and roll up, starting at the large side of triangle.
Dip in melted butter and let rise in a warm place 3-4 hours. Bake at 450° for 7-10 minutes. Dough will keep in refrigerator up to 10 days.

Homemade rolls without a lot of effort.

MONKEY BREAD

1 cup warm water
2 pkgs. dry yeast
1 cup boiling water
¾ cup sugar
1 cup shortening
2 tsp. salt
2 eggs
6 cups flour
1½ sticks margarine, melted

Dissolve yeast in warm water. Dissolve sugar, shortening and salt in boiling water. Cool, then add to yeast mixture. Beat in eggs and flour - let rise until doubled. Punch down and pinch off pieces. Dip in melted margarine and place in tube pan. Bake at 350° for 35-45 minutes.

Men really seem to enjoy this!

Leftovers are great warmed up for breakfast with jam. (We rarely have any left at our house though.)

WHEAT BREAD

1 tsp. sugar
2 pkgs. dry yeast
3 Tbsp. honey
1 cup powdered milk
2 cups hot water
1 Tbsp. salt
1 cup lukewarm water
3 Tbsp. oil
1 Tbsp. butter flavoring
4 cups whole wheat flour
4 cups white flour

Put 1 cup lukewarm water, sugar and yeast in a 2 cup container. Mix and let bubble to fill container (warm oven is great for this). Dissolve oil, honey, butter flavoring, powdered milk and 2 cups wheat flour in hot water (measure oil first, then butter and honey won't stick to the spoon; mix the powdered milk with flour so it won't lump). Beat these ingredients well. Add dissolved yeast, beat again, then let rise in a warm place until very bubbly (warm oven). Add salt, then beat in 2 cups wheat flour. Beating brings out the gluten and lets it rise and helps wet the flour. Whole wheat flour does not absorb moisture as well as white flour.

Knead in white flour and let rise until double in bulk. Knead dough until it loses its' flabby feeling and becomes firm and elastic.

Make out in 3 loaves, let rise until double in bulk.

Bake at 400° for 10 minutes, then 350° for 30 minutes.

ONION BREAD

1 pkg. active dry yeast
½ cup warm water
1 cup creamed cottage cheese,
  heated to lukewarm
2 Tbsp. sugar
1 Tbsp. butter
1 Tbsp. instant minced onion
2 tsp. dill seed
1 tsp. salt
½ tsp. soda
1 unbeaten egg
2¼-2½ cups flour

Soften yeast in water. Combine cottage cheese, sugar, onion, butter, dill seed, salt, soda, egg and softened yeast. Add flour to form a stiff dough, beating well after each addition. (For first addition, use mixer on low speed.)

Cover. Let rise in warm place (85° - 90°) until light and doubled in size (50-60 minutes). Stir down dough. Turn into well-greased loaf pans. Let rise 30-40 minutes. Bake at 350° for 40-50 minutes until golden brown. Brush with soft butter.

Makes two loaves 8½ x 4½ x 2½ or 2 (1 lb.) coffee cans, greased and lined with waxed paper. Baking in coffee cans gives a pretty and moist loaf.

This bread is great anytime, but it's especially good with soups and stews.

SOUR CREAM ONION BREAD

2 cups flour
1 pkg. dry yeast
½ cup sliced green onions with
  tops
2 Tbsp. butter
½ cup sour cream
⅓ cup milk
2 Tbsp. sugar
1 tsp. salt
1 egg

In mixer bowl, stir together 1 cup of flour and the yeast. In a saucepan, cook onion in butter until tender. Stir in sour cream, milk, sugar and salt. Heat slowly to lukewarm (110°-115°). Add to dry ingredients in mixer bowl along with egg. Beat at low speed of electric mixer for ½ minute scraping sides of bowl. Beat 3 minutes at high speed. By hand, stir in remaining flour. Spoon batter into a greased 1 quart casserole. Cover, let rise in a warm place about 1 hour until doubled. Bake at 375° for 35-40 minutes; cover with foil after 15 minutes to prevent over-browning. Cool 10 minutes - remove - serve warm.

CORN LIGHT BREAD

2 cups plain corn meal
¾ cup flour
¾ cup sugar
1 tsp. soda
1 tsp. salt
2 cups buttermilk
¼ cup oil or melted margarine
1 egg

Mix dry ingredients, add buttermilk, egg and oil. Pour batter into a greased loaf pan. Bake at 350° for 1 hour. Remove from oven and cool in pan for 30 minutes.
Refrigerate, if kept over 24 hours.

A sweet cornbread.

GRANDMOTHER'S CORNBREAD

. 2 cups white cornmeal
½ cup flour
½ tsp. soda
2 tsp. (heaping) baking powder
¼ cup oil
1 tsp. salt
1 egg
2 cups buttermilk
2 Tbsp. sugar

Combine all ingredients by hand. Pour into hot, greased iron skillet. Bake at 425° for 20 minutes.

Grandmother made cornbread every day when she visited us. She insisted it had to be eaten as soon as it came out of the oven and you had to have lots of butter on it. By the time we sat down to eat, most of the cornbread was gone. Boy, talk about good!

"THE BEST" HUSHPUPPIES

1 cup flour
1 cup cornmeal
1 tsp. salt
1½ Tbsp. baking powder
2 Tbsp. (heaping) sugar
1 egg
1 medium purple onion, chopped
1-1¼ cups hot milk

Mix all ingredients with milk; mixture should be just thin enough so that it will easily slide off a large spoon into grease. Fry in deep fat at 350° until golden-brown. These hushpuppies look puffy, like fritters.

Everytime we fix them, we are asked for the recipe. Bet you can't eat just one!

JALAPENO CORNBREAD

2½ cups cornmeal
1 cup flour
1½ tsp. salt
1 tsp. soda
4 tsp. baking powder
3 Tbsp. sugar
3 eggs, beaten
2¼ cups milk
½ cup oil
4-5 slices bacon - fried crisp and
  crumbled
Small jar chopped pimentos
1½ cups grated cheese
1 large onion, finely chopped
★Jalapenos to taste

Mix all ingredients together and pour into a hot greased pan (9x13). Bake at 450° for 30-40 minutes or until brown. Can be frozen. Makes 20 squares.

Unless you like really hot food, use only 2 jalapenos. Very good!

ZUCCHINI NUT BREAD

5 eggs
1½ cups oil
2 tsp. vanilla
1 Tbsp. lemon juice
1¼ cups sugar
3 cups flour
1 tsp. salt
½ tsp. nutmeg
1 Tbsp. cinnamon
1½ tsp. baking powder
2 tsp. baking soda
1 cup chopped pecans
¼ cup white raisins
2½ cups finely grated zucchini
Egg wash (1 whole egg mixed
  with ¼ cup milk)

Preheat oven to 350°. Combine eggs, oil, vanilla and lemon juice. In a separate bowl, mix sugar, flour, salt, nutmeg, cinnamon, baking powder, baking soda, nuts, raisins and zucchini. Gradually add dry ingredients to liquid. Beat until smooth. Grease and flour 2 loaf pans. Divide mixture evenly. Bake at 350° for 50 minutes. When bread is nearly done, brush with egg wash and return to oven until done.

We like someone because,
we love someone although.

POPPY SEED LOAF BREAD

3 cups flour
1½ tsp. salt
1½ tsp. baking powder
3 eggs
2¼ cups sugar
1⅛ cups oil
1½ cups milk
1½ Tbsp. poppy seed
1½ tsp. almond flavoring
1½ tsp. vanilla flavoring
1½ tsp. butter flavoring

Frosting:
¼ cup orange juice
¾ cup powdered sugar
½ tsp. butter flavoring
½ tsp. almond flavoring
½ tsp. vanilla flavoring

Mix all ingredients together for 2 minutes with an electric mixer. Bake in 2 greased loaf pans at 350° for 65 minutes. Cool 5 minutes and frost in pan.

Frosting:
Mix well and pour over loaves in pan. Let stand 10 minutes and remove from pans.

This is absolutely wonderful!

ORANGE PECAN BREAD

3 cups sifted flour
¾ cup sugar
2 tsp. baking powder
½ tsp. soda
1 tsp. salt
1 egg, lightly beaten
¼ cup melted butter
1 cup milk
½ cup orange juice
1 Tbsp. grated orange peel
1 cup chopped pecans

Sift flour again with sugar, baking powder, soda and salt. Add egg, melted butter, milk, orange juice and peel to the dry mixture. Stir just until all of flour mixture is moistened. Stir in pecans. Pour into greased loaf pan. Bake at 350° for about 1 hour and 10 minutes or until tests done. Let stand 10 minutes, then turn out onto wire rack.

BANANA BREAD I

½ cup margarine
2 cups sugar
3 eggs
2 cups flour
1½ tsp. soda
¼ tsp. salt
6 Tbsp. sour milk
4 bananas, mashed
1½ cups chopped pecans
1 tsp. vanilla

Cream together the margarine, sugar and eggs. Add flour, soda, salt and sour milk (*sour milk - use 1 teaspoon vinegar to ½ cup milk*). Add bananas, pecans and vanilla. Pour into 3-one pound coffee cans (greased and floured). Bake at 350° for 1 hour.

BANANA BREAD II

1 stick margarine
¾ cup sugar
1 egg
1 cup All-Bran
¾ cup chopped pecans
1½ cups mashed bananas
2 Tbsp. water
1½ tsp. vanilla
1½ cups flour
1½ tsp. baking powder
½ tsp. soda
½ tsp. salt

Cream together the margarine and sugar. Add egg and beat well. Add All-Bran and nuts. Add mashed bananas, water and vanilla. Mix together the flour, baking powder, soda and salt, add to the banana mixture and mix well. Put in a greased and floured loaf pan. Bake at 350° for 45-55 minutes.

MOTHER DORMER'S BANANA BREAD

2 eggs, beaten
½ cup oil
⅔ cup sugar
½ tsp. salt
3 large bananas
1¾ cups flour
⅓ tsp. soda
2 tsp. baking powder
1 tsp. vanilla
½ cup chopped pecans

Mix oil and sugar. Sift together flour, salt, baking powder and soda. Mash bananas and add to beaten eggs. Add this to the oil and sugar. Add dry ingredients and mix well. Add vanilla and nuts, mix. Pour into a buttered loaf pan. Bake at 350° for 1 hour.

This always makes going home a special treat.

CREAM CHEESE BREAD

1 cup sour cream
½ cup sugar
1 tsp. salt
½ cup melted butter
2 pkgs. dry yeast
½ cup warm water
2 eggs, beaten
4 cups flour

Filling:
2 (8 oz) pkgs. cream cheese
¾ cup sugar
1 egg, beaten
⅛ tsp. salt
2 tsp. vanilla

Heat sour cream on low heat; stir in sugar, salt and butter - cool. Sprinkle yeast over warm water in a large mixing bowl, stirring until yeast dissolves. Add sour cream mixture, eggs and flour; mix well. Cover tightly and refrigerate overnight. Next day, divide dough into 4 equal parts, roll each part out on a floured surface into a 12x8 rectangle. Spread ¼ of the filling on each rectangle. Roll up jelly-roll fashion, beginning at long sides. Pinch edges together and fold ends under slightly. Place the rolls, seam side down, on greased baking sheets. Cover and let rise in a warm place until doubled, about an hour.

Filling:
Combine cream cheese and sugar in a small mixing bowl. Add egg, salt and vanilla, mix well. Makes 2 cups. Bake at 375° for 12-15 minutes. Makes 4 loaves.

APPLE KUCHEN

1 yellow cake mix
1 stick margarine
1 can sliced apples
½ cup sugar
1 tsp. cinnamon
1 cup sour cream
1 egg

Cut margarine into cake mix until crumbly. Pat into a 9x13 pan. Bake at 350° for 10 minutes.
Spread apple slices over crust. Mix sugar and cinnamon, sprinkle over apples. Mix sour cream and egg, dribble over apples. Bake at 325° for 25 minutes.

Great for breakfast or brunch! Very rich.

 A friend in need is a friend in deed.

COFFEE BREAD

¼ cup margarine
¾ cup shortening
½ cup sugar
1 Tbsp. salt
2 eggs
2 pkgs. yeast
2 cups milk, scalded
6 cups flour
¼ cup melted margarine
Filling of your choice, recipe follows

Cream together the margarine, shortening, sugar and salt. Add eggs and yeast; mix well. Add milk and flour alternately. Brush top of dough with melted margarine. Let stand in a warm place until doubled (about 1 hour). Divide in half and roll out to about ¼" thickness in rectangle. Spread with melted margarine and filling. Roll up like a jelly roll and seal edges. Form into a circle on a cookie sheet sprayed with Pam. Let rise 1 hour. Bake at 350° for 30-35 minutes.
Makes 2.

FILLINGS:

Pineapple:
1 small can crushed pineapple
1 Tbsp. cornstarch
¼ cup sugar

Cook until thickened. Cool before putting on dough.
Makes enough for 1 loaf.

Cinnamon-Pecan:
1 Tbsp. cinnamon
¼ cup chopped pecans
¼ cup brown sugar

Mix and sprinkle on dough.
Makes enough for 1 loaf.

Date-nut:
1 cup chopped dates
½ cup chopped pecans
1 Tbsp. cornstarch
½ cup sugar

Cook until dates are melted. Cool before putting on dough.
Makes enough for 1 loaf.

Apricot:
1 cup cooked apricot
½ cup brown sugar
½ cup chopped pecans

Cook until thick. Cool before putting on dough.
Makes enough for 1 loaf.

BLUEBERRY COFFEECAKE

¾ cup sugar
¼ cup shortening
1 egg
½ cup milk
2 cups (less 1 Tbsp.) flour
2 tsp. baking powder
½ tsp. salt
2 cups blueberries (fresh or
  frozen, drained)

Topping:
½ cup sugar
⅓ cup flour
½ tsp. cinnamon
¼ cup soft butter
¼ cup chopped pecans

Grease and flour 9" square pan. Mix sugar, egg and shortening thoroughly. Stir in milk, flour, baking powder and salt. Fold in blueberries and pour into pan.

Combine topping ingredients and sprinkle over top of batter. Bake at 375° for 45-50 minutes. Serve warm.

SOUR CREAM COFFEECAKE

2 sticks butter
2 cups cake flour
2 cups sugar
3 eggs
1 cup sour cream
1 tsp. vanilla
Pinch salt
Pinch soda

Filling:
¼ cup brown sugar
1 tsp. cinnamon
¼ cup chopped pecans

Cream butter and sugar; add eggs. Beat well. Add flour, sour cream, soda, salt and vanilla. Beat well.

Mix brown sugar, cinnamon and pecans together. Grease a bundt pan. Sprinkle ½ of filling on bottom of pan. Pour in ½ of batter. Sprinkle remaining filling, then remaining batter. Bake at 350° for 1 hour.

One of the Absolute Best!

CINNAMON ROLLS

3½-4 cups flour
1 pkg. dry yeast
1¼ cups milk
¼ cup shortening
¼ cup sugar
1 tsp. salt
1 egg
¼ cup melted margarine
½ cup sugar
2 tsp. cinnamon
1½ cups powdered sugar
¼ tsp. vanilla
3-4 Tbsp. half and half
  (can use milk)

Put 2 cups flour and yeast in mixer bowl. Heat together milk, shortening, sugar and salt until shortening is melted. Add to flour with egg. Mix with mixer for 30 seconds on low, then 3 minutes on medium. Stir in 1½-2 cups flour to form dough. Let rise 2-3 hours. Divide dough in half. Roll out on floured surface in a rectangle.

Mix together melted margarine, ½ cup sugar and cinnamon. Spread ½ of this mixture on dough. Roll into a jelly roll. Slice into 12 rolls. Place into a 9x13 pan. Repeat, let rise 1-2 hours. Bake at 350° for 20-25 minutes.

Mix together powdered sugar, vanilla and milk, spread on rolls.

I always forget the egg when making these for Sam - they still turn out great. Mary always remembers the egg.

ORANGE MUFFINS

1 stick margarine
1 cup sugar
2 eggs
2 cups flour
1 tsp. salt
1 tsp. soda
1 cup buttermilk
⅔ cup white raisins
1 cup chopped pecans
2½ cups powdered sugar
½ cup orange juice
½ tsp. grated orange rind

Cream together margarine, sugar and eggs. Sift together flour, salt and soda; add alternately with buttermilk to creamed mixture. Stir in raisins and pecans. Pour into miniature muffin tins ⅔ full. Bake at 375° for 12 minutes.

Mix together the powdered sugar, orange juice and rind. Dip hot muffins into juice mixture. Cool on wax paper.

These muffins freeze beautifully!

Gwen would bring these to share while we had coffee and discussed what made our children tick. Those talks helped me more than anything when it came to dealing with my boys.

APPLE PANCAKE

3 eggs
½ cup milk
1 tsp. sugar
½ cup flour
¼ cup butter
1 large apple
Dash salt
Nutmeg

Topping:
¼ cup sugar
½ tsp. cinnamon
Butter

Mix together the eggs, milk, sugar, flour and salt. Melt butter in a large iron skillet. Peel and slice apple, fry in butter 3-4 minutes. Swirl butter around pan and up sides to coat. Pour batter over apples and sprinkle with nutmeg. Bake at 500° for 5 minutes.
Mix together ¼ cup sugar, ½ teaspoon cinnamon and sprinkle on top. Dot with butter and return to oven for 3-4 minutes.
Cut in wedges.

MACADAMIA NUT PANCAKES

1 cup flour
1 Tbsp. sugar
½ tsp. salt
1½ tsp. baking powder
½ tsp. soda
1 egg
1 cup buttermilk
1 Tbsp. oil
¼ cup chopped macadamia
  nuts

Mix all ingredients, except nuts, with an electric beater or in blender. Sprinkle each pancake with nuts while they are on the griddle.

COCONUT SYRUP

Small can coconut syrup
½ cup water
1 cup sugar
2 Tbsp. honey

Heat and serve warm with pancakes.

These are also good if you substitute blueberries for the nuts.

A friend is a present you give yourself.

Soup 'n Salads

CHEDDAR CHEESE SOUP

6 Tbsp. butter
¾ cup minced onion
¾ cup peeled and minced
  carrot
½ cup minced celery
1 tsp. minced garlic
4 Tbsp. flour
½ tsp. salt
¼ tsp. white pepper
½ tsp. paprika
Pinch cayenne
4½ cups chicken broth
1 cup whipping cream
2 Tbsp. white wine
3 cups sharp cheddar cheese,
  grated
¼ cup chopped parsley

In large pan, heat butter and saute onion, carrots, celery and garlic for 8-10 minutes. Sprinkle in flour and seasonings, blending well. Gradually add broth, stirring constantly, until thick and smooth. Reduce to simmer and add cream and wine. Gradually add cheese. Sprinkle with parsley and serve at once. Serves 4.

Great served in soup buns!

OYSTER SOUP

2 qts. milk
3 dozen oysters and water
1 bunch green onions,
  chopped
2 sticks butter
½ bunch parsley, chopped
Salt, if needed

Fry green onions in butter on low heat until tender. Add oyster water and let it come to a boil. Add parsley and milk, stirring constantly, then oysters. Cook until oysters curl - do not let milk boil (it will curdle) - take it off the burner just before boiling point. Serve with crackers.

Oyster Soup was a Christmas Eve tradition with my husband's family in New Orleans. Sandwiches were usually served as well.
We have it in the winter for supper with a salad or sandwich. Very good - very easy!

CLAM CHOWDER

6 slices bacon, chopped
1 medium onion, chopped
6 Tbsp. butter, divided
3 (6½ oz) cans minced clams
2 (10¾ oz) cans cream of potato soup
2 soup cans milk
Salt, pepper to taste
⅛ tsp. garlic powder
2 green onions, finely chopped

Saute bacon and onion in 3 tablespoons butter until onion is soft. Add clams and juice - simmer for 3 minutes. Add soup, then slowly add milk, stirring constantly. Add salt, pepper and garlic. Heat - do not boil. Just before serving, stir in 3 tablespoons butter and green onions.
Serves 8.

VEGETABLE BEEF SOUP

1½ lbs. ground chuck
1 cup chopped onion
1 cup chopped celery
½ cup chopped parsley
¼ tsp. cumin
¼ tsp. oregano
¼ tsp. marjoram
¼ tsp. tarragon
¼ tsp. sweet basil
Salt and pepper to taste
2 (12 oz) cans tomato juice
3 large potatoes, cubed
1 pkg. frozen corn
1 pkg. frozen peas
1 pkg. frozen lima beans
1½ cups grated carrots

Optional: grated turnips or zucchini

Brown meat with onions, celery and parsley. Add salt and pepper to taste with other seasoning. Add tomato juice and simmer. Cook potatoes in salted water until tender. Partially cook the frozen vegetables (I use the microwave). Add potatoes, vegetables and carrots to meat mixture and simmer. (Also add turnips or zucchini if desired). You may need more tomato juice.

Another good recipe from Mom!

 The best gifts are tied with heart-strings.

CREAM OF ARTICHOKE SOUP

2½ sticks butter
1 cup chopped carrot
1 cup chopped onion
1 cup chopped celery
1 cup chopped mushrooms
½ cup flour
2 cups chicken broth
4 (8½ oz) cans artichoke
  hearts, quartered (save juice)
2 bay leaves
1½ tsp. salt
1½ tsp. pepper
½ tsp. cayenne
1 tsp. thyme
1 tsp. oregano
½ tsp. sage
½ tsp. paprika
2 cups whipping cream

Melt ½ stick butter in large saucepan over medium heat. Add carrots, celery, onion and mushrooms and saute until vegetables are soft (10-15 min.) Set aside.

Melt 2 sticks butter in large stock pot over low heat. Add flour and cook, stirring constantly, 5 minutes. Stir in vegetables, add broth slowly, stirring constantly. Add artichoke hearts with juice and seasonings, stir. Increase heat to medium and simmer 30 minutes, stirring occasionally. Beat cream in small bowl just until frothy. Blend into soup. Heat through but **do not boil.** Adjust seasoning. In batches, put in processor. Process just until artichokes are finely chopped and blended. Serve immediately. Good made a day ahead, but add whipping cream just before serving.
Serves 8.

Excellent soup!

CREAM OF SPINACH SOUP

1 stick butter
2 Tbsp. bacon drippings
1 large onion, finely chopped
4 (10 oz) pkgs. frozen chopped
  spinach, thawed (save juice)
6 Tbsp. flour
2 (14½ oz) cans chicken
  broth
4 cups half and half
1½ tsp. white pepper
⅛ tsp. cayenne
½ tsp. fresh grated nutmeg
1 lb. bacon, chopped and
  cooked crisp
2 cups grated cheddar cheese

Melt butter and drippings in 4 qt. pot over medium heat. Add onion and cook about 5 minutes. Press spinach in large strainer, saving liquid. Add spinach to onion, mix well - add flour. Cook, stirring frequently, about 3 minutes. Blend in broth and spinach liquid - bring to simmer. Cook 10 minutes. Stir in half and half, pepper, and nutmeg - simmer 5 minutes. Add bacon and cheese. Ladle into bowls. Serve hot.
Serves 6-8.

CREAM OF MUSHROOM SOUP

¼ lb. butter
½ lb. sliced mushrooms
1 chopped onion
1 pt. chicken broth
1 pt. milk
½ pt. half and half
¼ cup flour
⅛ tsp. thyme
¼ tsp. oregano
¼ tsp. basil
1 bay leaf
Salt and pepper to taste

Saute onions and mushrooms in butter. Add flour; mix well. Add broth, milk and seasonings. Cook for 30 minutes on low heat, stirring often. Add half and half; heat through.
Serves 4.

SPINACH SALAD

Salad:
2 (10 oz) pkgs. fresh spinach, washed and dried
4 hard-boiled eggs, diced
8 strips bacon, fried crisp and crumbled
½ cup chopped green onions
8 oz pkg. mushrooms, sliced

Dressing:
1 cup oil (light)
5 Tbsp. red wine vinegar
4 Tbsp. sour cream
1½ tsp. salt
½ tsp. dry mustard
2 Tbsp. sugar
½ tsp. coarsely ground black pepper
¼ tsp. garlic powder
1 Tbsp. chopped parsley

Mix dressing at least 6 hours before using. Toss spinach with mushrooms and green onions. Add desired amount of dressing and toss well. Top with eggs and bacon.
Serves 6-8.

Even those who don't enjoy salad like this.

LAYERED SALAD

4 cups chopped lettuce
2½ cups grated Monterey Jack
   cheese ★
5 boiled eggs, sliced
1 lb. frozen peas, thawed and
   drained
3 cups torn fresh spinach
6 green onions, chopped
1 lb. bacon, cooked and
   crumbled
½ lb. fresh mushrooms, sliced
Salt and pepper
½ tsp. sugar

Dressing:
1¼ cups sour cream
½ cup mayonnaise
½ pkg. Italian salad dressing
   mix

★ Can use half Monterey and
half cheddar

Dry the lettuce and spinach well. Use a large glass bowl. Layer the lettuce in bottom of bowl, sprinkle with salt, pepper and sugar. Place some of the egg slices around sides of bowl, chop remaining and sprinkle over lettuce. Sprinkle 1 cup of cheese next. Layer the peas, then spinach, green onions, mushrooms, ¾ of the bacon and remaining cheese.

Mix together the sour cream, mayonnaise and Italian dressing mix. Spead over the top of salad, sealing completely. Cover and refrigerate overnight. Garnish with remaining bacon, green onions and a sprinkle of paprika. Toss at serving.

MEXICAN SALAD

1 large head lettuce
1 lb. grated cheddar cheese
15 oz can Ranch Style beans,
   chilled
2 large tomatoes, diced
1 small onion, chopped or
   6 green onions, chopped
¾-1 bottle Kraft Catalina
   dressing
1 medium bag Fritos, crushed
Salt and pepper to taste

Prepare lettuce as for tossed salad. Drain beans and add to lettuce. Add cheese, tomatoes, onion and dressing. Chill. Immediately before serving, add Fritos and seasonings.
Serves 12.

TACO SALAD MEAL

1 lb. ground meat
½ onion, chopped
½ tsp. minced garlic
1 envelope Taco seasoning
1 small can tomato paste
1 small can Ranch Style beans
4 cups torn lettuce
1 tomato, chopped
3 green onions, chopped
2 cups grated cheddar or Monterey Jack cheese
Hidden Valley Ranch dressing (mixed as directed)
Picante sauce to taste

Brown meat with onion and garlic; drain. Add Taco seasoning as directed on package. Simmer. Add tomato paste and ranch beans, simmer 15-20 minutes. Combine lettuce, tomato and green onions. When ready to serve, pour meat mixture over lettuce salad, cover with cheese. Top with dressing and picante sauce. Make these individually, rather than 1 large salad unless it will all be eaten at once. Serves 4-6.

A salad men love!

HELEN'S ONION RING SALAD

2 large onions, sliced
¼ cup vinegar
½ cup sugar
1 cup mayonnaise
1 Tbsp. celery seed or celery salt

Place onions in a bowl and pour mixture of vinegar and sugar over top. Add water to cover. Put in refrigerator for at least 30 minutes. Drain. When ready to serve, fold in 1 cup mayonnaise, mixed with celery seed.

Good with fish!

TROPICAL CHICKEN SALAD

★ 1 chicken, cooked and cubed (I use 4 chicken breasts)
1 large can pineapple tidbits, reserve liquid
1 cup chopped celery
1 head lettuce, torn as for tossed salad
1 cup coconut
¼-½ cup sliced almonds
1 cup Miracle Whip, thin with pineapple juice

Toast coconut and almonds in oven. Toss all ingredients together. Also good to add halved green grapes.
Serves 6-8.

★ I sprinkle on salt, pepper, garlic powder and soy sauce when I bake my chicken.

This is very good, don't let the variety of ingredients turn you off. Men really like this, too.

CAULIFLOWER - PEA SALAD

2 cups raw cauliflower flowerets (bite size)
2 cups raw broccoli flowerets (bite size)
4 green onions, chopped
1 cup frozen green peas, thawed
½ cup bacon bits

Dressing:
¾ cup mayonnaise
½ cup sour cream
½ tsp. salt
½ tsp. garlic powder
¼ tsp. pepper

Mix dressing ingredients and refrigerate over night. Just before serving, combine cauliflower, broccoli, onions and peas in a large bowl. Toss the vegetables with dressing and add bacon bits.
Serves 6-8.

FRUIT SALAD AND RUM DRESSING

1 cantaloupe, cubed
2 apples, diced
1 pt. strawberries, sliced
2 cups watermelon cubes
2 cups fresh pineapple, cubed
2 bananas, sliced
1 can mandarin oranges

Rum Dressing:
¾ cup brown sugar
1 tsp. dry mustard
1 tsp. salt
⅓ cup lime juice
1½ Tbsp. rum
1 cup oil (vegetable)

Combine fruits in a large bowl. In blender, add all dressing ingredients except oil; blend well. With machine running, slowly add oil. Chill. Pour over fruits and mix well. Will stay fresh for 2-3 days.
You can use your own combination of fruits if you desire.
Serves 6-8.

This dressing is one of Pam's specialties! I keep trying new ones but this is by far the best.

GLAZED FRUIT SALAD

4⅛ oz pkg. Jello instant pudding (banana, lemon, vanilla or French vanilla)
15¼ oz can pineapple chunks (drain and save liquid)
11 oz can mandarin oranges (drain and save liquid)
1 or 2 medium bananas, sliced
Fresh fruit (strawberries, peaches or apples)

In large bowl, add pudding mix. Mix liquids to equal one cup. Add to pudding and blend thoroughly. Add fruits.

Very easy and goes with anything.

WALDORF SALAD

1 cup mayonnaise
1 cup sour cream
2 Tbsp. honey
3 cups diced apples (I prefer Granny Smith)
1½ cups diced celery
1 cup chopped walnuts
¼ tsp. lemon juice

Combine apples, celery, lemon juice and walnuts in medium bowl. In a small bowl, blend mayonnaise, sour cream and honey. Add dressing to apple mixture and chill.
Serves 6-8.

NANCY'S STRAWBERRY PRETZEL SALAD

¾ cup margarine
3 Tbsp. brown sugar
2½ cups crushed pretzels
1 large pkg. strawberry jello
2 cups boiling water
3 cups chilled sliced strawberries
8 oz cream cheese
8 oz Cool Whip
½ cup sugar

Combine pretzels, brown sugar and margarine (melted). Mix well and pat in lightly buttered 9x13 pan. Bake at 350° for 10 minutes.
Dissolve jello in boiling water. While still hot, add berries. Cool until it begins to set.
Meanwhile, beat cream cheese and sugar. Fold in cool whip. Spread cream cheese mixture over crust. Pour soft jello over cheese and chill.
Serves 10-12.
Delish!

PINEAPPLE PRETZEL SALAD
(Very Different)

1 stick margarine, melted
3 Tbsp. sugar
1 heaping cup of broken
  pretzels
8 oz pkg. cream cheese
½ cup sugar
2 cups Cool Whip
1 large can crushed pineapple,
  drained

Mix together melted margarine, 3 tablespoons sugar and pretzels. Put into a 9x13 pan and bake at 400° for 10 minutes. Take a spatula and loosen pretzels from bottom of pan. Cool.
Blend together cream cheese, ½ cup sugar, Cool Whip and drained pineapple. Spread on top of cooled pretzels. Refrigerate.
Serves 10-12.

Great for a salad luncheon. Barbara introduced me to this at a tennis luncheon; it's been a hit ever since.

PINEAPPLE - CHEESE SALAD

14 oz can crushed pineapple
2 cups liquid
1 (3 oz) pkg. lime jello
½ pkg., 3 oz lemon jello
4 oz cream cheese, softened
½ cup sour cream
¾ cup grated cheddar cheese
¾ cup cottage cheese

Drain pineapple, add water to syrup to make 2 cups. Heat to boiling. Place jello in large bowl and add 1 cup boiling liquid, stir to dissolve. Beat hot mixture into softened cream cheese. Add remaining liquid. Chill until partially thick.
In chilled bowl, with chilled beaters, add cheddar cheese, cottage cheese and pineapple to gelatin. Beat 5 minutes at high speed. Fold in sour cream. Pour into 9x13 pan and refrigerate until firm.

Great with bar-b-cue.

EDNA'S CRANBERRY SALAD

#2 can crushed pineapple
1 lb. fresh cranberries
1 envelope Knox unflavored
  gelatin
¼ cup water
1¾ cups sugar
1 cup chopped pecans

Drain pineapple 20-30 minutes. Boil juice and add cranberries. Cook until they stop popping. Remove from heat. Mix gelatin in water and add to cranberries. Stir well. Add sugar, crushed pineapple and pecans. Pour into a mold and refrigerate at least 6 hours.
Serves 8-10.

A must at Thanksgiving and Christmas!

CHICKEN SALAD

3½ cups diced chicken
1 Tbsp. lemon juice
1 Tbsp. peanut oil
½ tsp. salt
¼ tsp. pepper
⅛ tsp. cayenne
3 Tbsp. chopped green
  onions
6 slices bacon, cooked and
  crumbled
1 small can sliced black olives
2 cups chopped celery
1 Tbsp. sweet relish
¾ cup mayonnaise
¼ cup sour cream

Combine chicken, lemon juice, oil, green onions and seasonings. Cover and refrigerate overnight. Add bacon, olives, celery, relish, mayonnaise and sour cream. Mix well and serve stuffed in tomatoes or avocado halves on a lettuce leaf.
Serves 6-8.

HOT CHICKEN SALAD

2 cups diced,cooked chicken
½ cup slivered almonds,
  toasted
¼ cup finely chopped onion
1½ cups chopped celery
2 tsp. lemon juice
½ tsp. salt
¼ tsp. pepper
1 cup mayonnaise

Topping:
1 cup crushed potato chips
½ cup grated cheddar cheese

Combine all ingredients except topping. Place in a shallow baking dish (this much can be done ahead of time). Just before baking, sprinkle on topping. Bake at 400° for approximately 20 minutes, or until bubbly. Serve immediately.
Serves 4-6.

Great for luncheons, but if you take it, also take the recipe. You will have people ask for it.

A friend is one who comes to you
when all others leave.

TASTY TUNA SALAD

1 (6 oz) can light tuna in water
½ apple, diced
2 Tbsp. celery, diced
2 Tbsp. green onion, diced
1 Tbsp. sweet pickle relish
1 boiled egg, diced
4 Tbsp. Weight Watcher's
  mayonnaise
Salt and pepper to taste

Combine all ingredients and chill. Serve on a lettuce leaf. Garnish with cherry tomatoes, parsley and carrot sticks.

A light, refreshing lunch for two (low calorie).

WEST INDIES SALAD

1 lb. lump crabmeat
⅔ cup light oil
⅓ cup vinegar
½ cup chopped onion
½ tsp. garlic salt
¼ tsp. pepper
⅛ tsp. oregano
⅛ tsp. Italian seasoning
Juice of ½ lemon

Combine all ingredients and chill. Serve on a lettuce leaf or avocado half.

SHRIMP SALAD

1 cup mayonnaise
8 oz sour cream
1 pkg. Ranch dressing
8 oz pkg. small shell
  macaroni
1½-2 lbs. boiled shrimp
1 bunch green onions,
  chopped
3 stalks celery, chopped
1 carrot, grated
Salt and seasoned pepper
  to taste

Peel, devein and chop shrimp. Mix together the sour cream, mayonnaise and dressing mix. Cook macaroni, rinse and drain. Put macaroni in a large bowl, add ½ of dressing. Add salt and seasoned pepper to taste. Add shrimp, green onions, celery, carrots and ½ of the remaining dressing. Stir well and refrigerate over night. Before serving, add remaining dressing, stir well. Garnish with paprika and parsley. Serves 6-8.

This is always a big hit!

Eggs
And
Cheese

BETTY'S CRABMEAT OMELET

1 lb. lump crabmeat
5-6 green onions, chopped
3-4 cloves garlic, minced
½ bell pepper, chopped
¾ stick butter
1 tsp. seasoned pepper
1 tsp. salt
4-6 oz Swiss cheese, grated
8 eggs
½ cup half and half

In 10" skillet, melt butter and saute onions, bell pepper and garlic. Add crabmeat and simmer a few minutes. Put eggs, half and half, salt and pepper in blender; blend on high for 40-60 seconds. Pour over crab mixture and sprinkle on cheese. Cover and cook over medium heat for 10-12 minutes. Remove from skillet to a plate and flip over into skillet, cook another 10-12 minutes. Remove to plate and cut into wedges to serve.
Serves 6.

Mother whipped this up one morning at 6 a.m. while I followed her around with my paper and pencil. Neither of my parents measures anything!

BREAKFAST PIZZA

1 lb. roll bulk sausage
1 pkg. refrigerated crescent rolls
1 cup frozen hash browns, thawed
1 cup grated cheddar cheese
5 eggs
¼ cup milk
½ tsp. salt
¼ tsp. pepper
⅛ tsp. paprika
⅛ tsp. garlic powder
2 Tbsp. Parmesan cheese

Break up sausage and cook. Drain. Separate rolls and place on an ungreased pizza pan to form crust, sealing edges. Spoon on sausage, potatoes and cheese. Beat eggs, milk and seasonings together. Pour over crust. Sprinkle with Parmesan cheese. Bake at 375° for 25-30 minutes.
Serves 6.

The Father is the head of the house, the Mother is the heart of the house.

SAUSAGE BRUNCH

12 slices bread, crusts removed
2-3 Tbsp. soft margarine
½ cup margarine
½ lb. sliced mushrooms
1 cup chopped onion
1 cup chopped green onion
1½ tsp. minced garlic
Salt, pepper to taste
1½ lb. bulk hot sausage
¾ lb. grated cheddar cheese
5 eggs
2½ cups milk
1 Tbsp. Dijon mustard
1 tsp. dry mustard
1 tsp. ground nutmeg
2 Tbsp. chopped parsley
1 tsp. salt
¼ tsp. pepper

Butter one side of bread with soft margarine and set aside. Melt ½ cup margarine and saute onions, green onions, garlic and mushrooms until tender. Add salt and pepper to taste. Cook sausage and drain well. In a greased baking dish, layer ½ the bread, butter side down. Add ½ the sausage-onion mixture and ½ of the grated cheese. Repeat. In a bowl, beat together the eggs, milk, mustard, nutmeg, salt and pepper. Pour over sausage and bread. Cover and refrigerate overnight. Set out until room temperature. Sprinkle with parsley. Bake uncovered at 350° for 1 hour.
Serves 6-8.

SPECIAL MORNING CASSEROLE

4 slices bacon
12 oz sliced ham, cubed
4 oz jar sliced mushrooms
1 bell pepper, chopped
1 stick butter, divided
3 green onions, chopped
½ cup flour
1 qt. milk
½ tsp. pepper
16 eggs
1 cup evaporated milk
Salt to taste
6-8 drops Tabasco (optional)

Saute bacon and remove from skillet. Add ham, mushrooms (reserve some for garnish), bell pepper and ½ stick butter to bacon drippings. Stir in flour, milk, green onions, and pepper. Cook slowly until mixture thickens to a cream sauce consistency. Mix eggs with evaporated milk, season with salt and Tabasco. Scramble eggs in remaining butter. In a 3 quart casserole, alternate layers of sauce and eggs beginning and ending with sauce. Eggs must be completely covered with sauce. Garnish with mushrooms. Bake covered at 275° for one hour. May be made a day ahead and refrigerated.
Serves 12.

BRUNCH EGGS

16 slices white bread
16 oz grated sharp cheddar
  cheese
1 lb. bacon or sausage, cooked
½ cup green onions, chopped
½ cup chopped onions
1 can Rotel tomatoes
½ tsp. salt
¼ tsp. garlic powder
¼ tsp. black pepper
Dash cayenne
6 eggs, beaten
3 cups milk
1 tsp. dry mustard

Remove crusts from bread and butter one side. Arrange 8 slices, butter side down in baking dish. Cover with ½ of the cheese, then all of the meat, onions and Rotel tomatoes (drain and cut up). Sprinkle with seasonings. Repeat bread and top with remaining cheese. Mix eggs, milk and mustard well. Pour over and refrigerate overnight. Bake at 350° for 40 minutes.
Serves 8.

HAM BREAKFAST PUFF

2 cups diced ham
12 slices white bread
6 eggs, beaten
¾ lb. cheddar cheese, grated
3½ cups milk
¼ cup chopped onions
½ tsp. minced garlic
½ tsp. salt
¼ tsp. pepper
1 tsp. dry mustard
½ tsp. Worcestershire sauce
3-4 drops Tabasco

Grease 9x13 pan. Cut bread in circles. Save crusts and put in bottom of pan. Layer cheese on top (save some to sprinkle on top), then ham and bread circles. Beat together remaining ingredients and pour on top. Cover and refrigerate overnight. Bake at 325° for 55 minutes. Remove and add remaining cheese, bake 5 minutes more.
Serves 8.

EGGS FOR A BUNCH

¼ cup butter
1½ dozen eggs
1⅔ cups milk
1¼ tsp. salt
1 tsp. pepper
8 oz cream cheese, chopped

Melt butter in 9x13 pan. Mix together eggs, milk, salt and pepper. Pour into pan and bake at 350° for 20 minutes. Add cheese and stir well. Bake 8-10 minutes longer.
Serves 8-10.

ZUCCHINI AND EGGS

3 medium zucchini
1 onion, chopped
3-4 cloves garlic, minced
¼ lb. bacon, chopped
¼ lb. smoked sausage,
  chopped
¼ tsp. oregano
½ tsp. salt
¼ tsp. pepper
6 eggs, beaten

Wash zucchini and grate (leave peelings on). Saute bacon and sausage with oregano. Add onions and garlic; cook until wilted. Add zucchini, then eggs, salt and pepper. Cook over medium heat until done, stirring constantly. Serves 6.

Try it, you'll love it!
Another of Dad's creations.

CORN AND EGGS

1 can white shoepeg corn
6 green onions, chopped
4-5 cloves garlic, minced
½ stick butter
6 eggs, beaten
½ tsp. salt
¼ tsp. pepper

Saute onions and garlic in butter, add corn and cook until tender. Add eggs seasoned with salt and pepper. Cook and stir over medium heat until eggs are set.
Serves 4-6.

CHILI AND EGGS

★ 10-12 oz can chili (without
  beans)
1 onion, chopped
4-5 cloves garlic, minced
5 eggs, beaten with salt and
  pepper
2 Tbsp. butter

Saute onion and garlic in butter until tender. Add chili and simmer a few minutes. Add eggs seasoned with salt and pepper. Cook and stir over medium heat until done.

This is wonderful rolled up in flour tortillas with picante sauce on the side.
Serves 4.

★ *Great if you have leftover "homemade" chili.*

It's smart to pick your friends -
but not to pieces.

MINIATURE SAUSAGE QUICHE

★ 8 oz pkg. refrigerated
  butterflake rolls
½ lb. hot sausage
2 eggs, beaten
1 cup cottage cheese
3 green onions, chopped
¼ cup Parmesan cheese
Garlic salt, pepper and
  cayenne to taste

Separate rolls into 48 pieces. Press into greased miniature muffin tins. Brown sausage and drain. Spoon over dough. Mix eggs, cheese, onions and seasonings. Spoon over sausage. Bake at 375° for 20 minutes.

★ Sometimes these are hard to find; you can use refrigerated flaky biscuits.

JUBILEE JACK

1 (8 oz) pkg. sour cream
8 oz can tomato sauce
10 oz can Rotel tomatoes
Large bag Doritos
2 eggs
1 pt. half and half
1 small onion, chopped
½ tsp. salt
1 lb. Monterey Jack cheese,
  cubed
½ cup grated cheddar cheese
1 Tbsp. margarine

Saute onions in margarine. Add salt, tomato sauce and Rotel tomatoes (diced); simmer until bubbly. In a bowl, combine eggs and half and half; add to tomato mixture and simmer 5 minutes.
In 9x13 pan, put a layer of Doritos, cubed cheese and sauce. Repeat twice. Ice with sour cream, sprinkle with cheddar cheese. Stack a few Doritos around sides. Bake at 300° for 15 minutes.
Serves 4-6.

QUICHE LORRAINE

2 (9") pie shells
6 slices bacon, cooked and
  crumbled
1 bunch green onions,
  chopped
1 Tbsp. butter
1 (4 oz) jar sliced mush-
  rooms
½ cup shredded ham
1 cup grated swiss cheese
½ cup grated cheddar cheese
4 eggs
1½ cups evaporated milk
2-3 cloves minced garlic
½ tsp. salt
½ tsp. dry mustard
¼ tsp. black pepper
Dash nutmeg and cayenne

Prebake shells in 400° oven for 10 minutes. Saute onions in butter. Layer bacon, onions, mushrooms, ham and cheese in the two shells. Combine eggs with the remaining ingredients which have been beaten together. Pour custard in filled shells. Bake at 350° for 35 minutes or until a knife inserted in center comes out clean.
Serves 8.

CHILE-CHEESE SOUFFLE

1 lb. sharp cheddar cheese,
  grated
7 oz can chopped chiles
4 eggs
Pinch of soda
¼ tsp. salt
⅛ tsp. pepper
Dash cayenne

Butter a 1½ quart casserole. Cover with half the cheese. Add chiles, then remaining cheese. In blender, beat eggs with soda and seasonings. Pour over cheese. Bake at 400° for 35 minutes. Serve immediately with picante sauce.
Serves 4.

Vegetables

STUFFED ARTICHOKE BOTTOMS

1 can drained artichoke
  bottoms
1 pkg. Stouffer's frozen spinach
  souffle, thawed
Parmesan cheese
Garlic salt
Pepper
Paprika

Stuff the artichoke bottoms with thawed souffle. Arrange in a baking dish. Sprinkle each with
Parmesan cheese, garlic salt, pepper and paprika. Bake at 350° for 15 minutes.

Elegant looking but very easy!

ARTICHOKE CASSEROLE

1 can of crabmeat
2 cans Hearts of Artichokes
  (mashed)
6 oz olive oil
4 cloves garlic or garlic
  powder
¾ cup artichoke water
1 tsp. lemon juice
1 (3 oz) can Parmesan cheese
1 (8 oz) can Italian bread crumbs
Salt and pepper to taste

Combine all ingredients in a large casserole.
Bake at 350°, covered, for 30 minutes; then
uncover and bake an additional 10-15 minutes.
Serves 6-8.

BEAN-CARROT BAKE

2 cups green beans, cooked
2 cups diced carrots, cooked
6 Tbsp. butter
¼ cup finely chopped onion
4 Tbsp. flour
1½ cups milk
1 cup grated Velveeta Cheese
2 egg yolks
Salt, pepper and creole
  seasoning to taste
Italian bread crumbs

Make a sauce with melted butter and onion.
Cook until onion is transparent. Add flour,
gradually stir in milk. Add cheese, stirring constantly, until melted. Add egg yolks and seasonings, mix well. Mix vegetables together in a
casserole and pour sauce over them. Top with
bread crumbs. Bake at 300° for 30 minutes.
Serves 8-10.

FRENCH GREEN BEANS

2 Tbsp. butter
2 Tbsp. flour
1 tsp. salt
½ tsp. pepper
1 Tbsp. onion, chopped
1 tsp. sugar
¼ tsp. cayenne
1 cup sour cream
2 pkgs. frozen French-style
  green beans, cooked
½ cup grated cheddar cheese
1 cup crushed cornflakes
1 Tbsp. melted butter

Mix butter, flour, salt, pepper, onion, sugar, cayenne, sour cream and green beans. Put in buttered baking dish. Cover with mixture of cheese, cornflakes and melted butter. Bake at 400° for 20 minutes.
Serves 8-10.

LIMA BEAN BAKE

2 (10 oz) pkgs. frozen Ford-
  hook lima beans
10 slices bacon, diced
½ cup celery, chopped
1 large onion, chopped
1 cup shredded Monterey Jack
  cheese
1 cup shredded cheddar
  cheese
¾ tsp. black pepper
1½ tsp. Worcestershire sauce
½ tsp. garlic powder

Cook lima beans in 1½ cups boiling, salted water for 15 minutes; drain, reserve ½ cup liquid. Fry bacon, remove with slotted spoon and drain. Cook onion, celery and garlic in bacon drippings until wilted. Toss all ingredients together and put in a greased 2 quart casserole. Bake at 350° for 25-30 minutes.

Great for a bar-b-que or fish fry.

SPANISH GREEN BEANS

4 slices bacon, chopped
½ cup chopped onion
2 Tbsp. chopped bell pepper
Salt and pepper to taste
2 Tbsp. flour
1 lb. can stewed tomatoes
1 lb. can green beans
½ tsp. oregano
½ tsp. basil

Fry the bacon, onion and pepper in a skillet until bacon is crisp and onions and pepper are brown. Add flour, stir and add drained tomatoes and beans, season to taste. Add basil and oregano and place in casserole. Bake at 350° for 30 minutes.
Serves 4-6.

RANCH BEAN BAKE

1 lb. 7 oz can Ranch Style
beans
2 (15 oz) cans lima beans
2 (1 lb. 4 oz) can pork and
beans
1 large onion, chopped
½-1 tsp. garlic powder
8 slices bacon, cooked crisp
and crumbled (reserve
drippings)
¾ cup ketchup
1 tsp. soda
5 Tbsp. apple cider vinegar
5 Tbsp. brown sugar
1½ tsp. dry mustard
Salt, pepper to taste
5-6 drops of Tabasco

Saute onion and garlic in bacon drippings. Add all ingredients except bacon in a large casserole, mix well. Sprinkle bacon over top. Bake at 350° for 1 hour.

This can also be done in the microwave. Cook at full power for 12-15 minutes or until heated through and temperature of 150° is reached. Stir halfway through cooking time.
Serves 10-12.

Excellent for bar-b-ques.

ROBERTA'S BLACK BEANS

2 lbs. black beans
Water
3 large tomatoes
1 can tomato sauce
4 tsp. cumin
2 tsp. Worcestershire sauce
Salt, pepper to taste
Garlic powder
2 bay leaves
3 onions, chopped
1 large bell pepper, chopped
2 Tbsp. bacon grease

Saute onion and bell pepper in bacon grease until soft. Place remaining ingredients in large pan. Add enough water to cover 1" above beans. Add sauteed vegetables and cook slowly until done. May need to add more water. Serve over rice with chopped purple onion.
Dip:
Mash beans and fry in bacon grease until thick. Place in foil and freeze. To heat, place in 350° oven until hot. Top with sour cream and chopped green onions. Serve with tortilla chips or fritos.

Real friends are those who, when you've made
a fool of yourself, don't feel that you've
done a permanent job.

BROCCOLI - RICE CASSEROLE

1 stick margarine
1 rib of celery, chopped
1 onion, chopped
4 green onions, chopped
3-4 cloves garlic, minced
1 bunch fresh broccoli (may use frozen)
1 can Cream of Mushroom soup
1 small jar Jalapeno Cheese Whiz
2 cups cooked rice
3-4 drops Tabasco
½ tsp. salt
¼ tsp. pepper
4 Tbsp. bread crumbs

In a large skillet, saute celery, onion, green onions and garlic in margarine until clear. Cook broccoli until tender, drain well and cut into bite-size pieces. Mix broccoli with soup and cheese, add to vegetable mixture. Stir in rice and seasonings, mix well. Put into a greased casserole and top with bread crumbs. Bake at 350° for 45 minutes. Freezes very well. Serves 6-8.

CABBAGE AU GRATIN

1½-2 lbs. cabbage, chopped
Water to cover
3 Tbsp. butter
¼ cup flour
1 cup whipping cream
½ cup milk
1 tsp. salt
½ tsp. white pepper
¼ tsp. cayenne
3 Tbsp. butter (topping)
Bread crumbs
Grated Parmesan cheese

Cook cabbage in water until tender, about 7-8 minutes. Drain well. Melt butter, blend in flour, add cream and milk slowly, stirring constantly, until thickened. Stir in salt and peppers. Remove from heat and stir in cabbage. Pour into a buttered baking dish, dot with butter and sprinkle with cheese and bread crumbs. Bake at 375° for 20-25 minutes. Flavors blend better if made a day ahead.
Serves 8.

CARROT FRITTERS

1 lb. carrots
2 eggs
1 cup flour
1 tsp. garlic powder
5 green onions, chopped
1½ Tbsp. chopped parsley
1 Tbsp. sugar
Salt and pepper to taste

Heat oil for deep-frying in skillet. Peel and grate carrots fine. In a large mixing bowl, combine carrots, flour, eggs, garlic powder, onions, parsley, sugar, salt and pepper. Mix very well, with hands if necessary, until all ingredients are blended together. With a tablespoon, spoon carrot mixture into hot oil. Fry until brown. Serves 4-6.

These are yummy!

MIDGE'S CARROT TORTE

1¼ cups flour
½ tsp. soda
1 Tbsp. baking powder
1 Tbsp. nutmeg
1 Tbsp. cinnamon
Juice of 1 lemon
2 cups grated carrots
¾ cup brown sugar
½ cup butter
½ cup oil
2 eggs, separated
1 pkg. frozen peas with pearl onions, cooked

Combine brown sugar, oil and butter; beat in egg yolks. Add remaining ingredients, except egg whites and peas. Beat egg whites until stiff. Fold into above mixture. Pour into a greased ring mold. Bake at 350° for 25 minutes. Unmold and fill center with cooked peas and onions. Serve immediately.
Serves 4-6.

A very colorful dish; makes a festive side dish. Thanks, Midge!

CREAMED CAULIFLOWER

1 large head cauliflower
1 can Cream of Mushroom soup
¼ cup milk
½ cup sour cream
¼ cup toasted almonds
½ cup grated cheddar cheese

Steam cauliflower until tender, do not overcook. Heat the soup. Add sour cream and milk and heat again (do not boil). Pour sauce over drained cauliflower. Garnish with almonds and cheese.
Serves 6-8.

ZESTY CARROTS

2 lbs. carrots
1 large onion, chopped
8 slices bacon
1 tsp. salt
½ tsp. black pepper
1 tsp. sugar
Dash cayenne

Peel and slice carrots. Cook bacon until crisp and set aside. In a skillet, saute carrots and onion in bacon grease, sprinkle with seasonings. Cover and cook slowly about 15-20 minutes or until barely tender; uncover and cook until slightly browned, stirring occasionally. Crumble bacon and add to carrots. Serve immediately.
Serves 8.

Even my brother, Joey, will eat carrots fixed this way. The bacon and onion really add a special flavor.

EGGPLANT CASSEROLE
(Casserole or Hot Appetizer)

1 large (or 2 small) eggplants
1 small onion, chopped
10 slices bacon
1 lb. ground beef
1 large chopped onion
1 clove garlic (or garlic powder)
1 stick margarine
1 large can (1 lb. 12 oz)
  stewed tomatoes
1½ cups cooked rice
1 cup Italian bread crumbs,
  (approx.)
Salt and pepper to taste

Peel and cube eggplant. Boil until tender in a little water with salt and small onion (just enough water to keep from sticking - stir often). Strain, save juice, and mash eggplant. Fry bacon until crisp, set aside. Saute large onion and garlic in margarine. Brown ground beef in bacon grease. Mix eggplant, salt, pepper, onion, crumbled bacon, ground meat, stewed tomatoes (drained and chopped), rice and bread crumbs. If too dry, add reserved juice. Simmer 20 minutes.

Casserole: Place in a greased dish. Top with bread crumbs. Bake at 350° for 20-30 minutes.

Appetizer: Serve hot in chafing dish with crackers (Triscuits best).

People who don't like eggplant love this! Don't tell them what it is and they'll rave. Sam always tells though; he loves it and this way he has more for himself.

CORN-RICE CASSEROLE

1 stick butter
1 onion, chopped
½ cup bell pepper
1 tsp. minced garlic
3 Tbsp. flour
2 Tbsp. chili sauce
1 can peeled tomatoes
1 tsp. salt
1 tsp. pepper
1 tsp. Worcestershire sauce
Dash Tabasco
1 can whole kernel corn
2 cups cooked rice
1 cup grated cheddar cheese

Melt butter and saute onion, bell pepper and garlic. Add flour, chili sauce and tomatoes (chopped). Blend well. Add salt, pepper, Worcestershire, Tabasco and corn. Add rice and pour into a greased casserole dish. Sprinkle cheese on top. Bake at 350° for 20 minutes. Serves 6.

To handle yourself, use your head; to handle others, use your heart.

CORN AND GREEN BEAN CASSEROLE

1 large can French-style green
  beans
1 can shoepeg corn
½ cup margarine
½ cup celery, chopped
½ cup onion, chopped
¼ cup bell pepper, chopped
1 tsp. minced garlic
1 small pkg. slivered almonds
1 can Cream of Celery soup
½ cup sour cream
½ cup grated cheddar cheese
¼ tsp. salt
¼ tsp. pepper
1 cup cheese crackers

Saute celery, onion, bell pepper, garlic and ½ package almonds in margarine. Add soup, sour cream, cheese, green beans, corn, salt and pepper. Place in a casserole dish. Sprinkle with remaining almonds. Crush cheese crackers and sprinkle on top. Bake at 350° for 45 minutes. Serves 6.

CORN PUDDING

2 eggs, beaten
Salt and pepper to taste
2 Tbsp. sugar
8 crushed buttery crackers
  (Escort)
3 Tbsp. soft butter
¼ cup evaporated milk
1 (1 lb.) can cream-style corn

Beat eggs; add salt, pepper, sugar, cracker crumbs, butter, milk and corn. Bake at 350° until puffed in center, about 45 minutes. Serves 4.

PINEAPPLE CASSEROLE

2 (20 oz) cans pineapple
  chunks
½ cup brown sugar
½ cup granulated sugar
6 Tbsp. flour
2 cups shredded sharp cheddar
  cheese
1 stick margarine, melted
1 cup Ritz crackers, crushed

Drain pineapple. Reserve 6 tablespoons juice. Mix flour and sugar; stir in reserved juice. Add pineapple and cheese. Place in a greased 2 quart casserole. Mix margarine and cracker crumbs, sprinkle on top. Bake at 350° for 30 minutes.
Serves 8-10.

Great for brunches and special meals!

BAKED FRUIT

1 (1 lb.) can sliced peaches
1 (1 lb.) can apricots
1 (1 lb.) can pears, sliced or cubed
1 (1 lb.) can pineapple chunks
1 small jar maraschino cherries
1 stick margarine
1 cup brown sugar, packed

Combine fruits, drained, in 2 quart casserole. Melt margarine and brown sugar. Pour over fruit and bake at 350° for 45 minutes.
Serves 6-8.

Good for brunch!

CHEESY POTATOES

1¼ cups milk
8 oz pkg. cream cheese, softened
2 Tbsp. green onions, chopped
1 Tbsp. onion, chopped
¼ tsp. salt
4 cups cubed, cooked potatoes (4 medium potatoes)
Paprika

In medium saucepan, blend milk into cream cheese over low heat. If necessary, beat with rotary beater. Stir in green onions, onion and salt. Add cubed potatoes; stir carefully to coat. Pour mixture into 1½ quart casserole and sprinkle with paprika. Bake at 350° for 30 minutes.
Serves 5-6.

CREAMY POTATOES

6 large potatoes
4 Tbsp. butter
8 oz sour cream
3 oz cream cheese
¾ tsp. salt
½ tsp. pepper
⅛ tsp. cayenne
Paprika

Peel, dice and boil potatoes until tender. Drain and whip with mixer. Add remaining ingredients and beat well. Pour into a buttered casserole and sprinkle with paprika. Bake at 350° for 15-20 minutes.
Serves 6.

My boys' favorite!

BAKED SHOESTRING POTATOES

4 medium baking potatoes
3 Tbsp. butter
1½ tsp. salt
Dash pepper
½ cup grated sharp cheddar
  cheese
2 Tbsp. chopped parsley
½ cup light or heavy cream
Aluminum foil

Cut a 48" length of foil; fold in half. Peel and cut potatoes as for fries; place just off center on foil. Dot with butter. Sprinkle with salt, pepper, cheese and parsley. Pull edges up, then pour cream over potatoes; seal. Cook over coals outside or place on shallow pan in oven and bake at 450° for 1 hour or until done.
Serves 4.

SWISS CREAMED PEAS

3 (10 oz) pkgs. frozen peas
2 cups sliced green onions
3 Tbsp. butter
2 Tbsp. flour
2 cups whipping cream
1 tsp. finely grated lemon peel
1½ cups grated Swiss cheese
½ tsp. salt (or to taste)

In a large saucepan, cook peas. Meanwhile, in a medium pan, cook onion in butter until tender. Blend in flour and ½ teaspoon salt; add cream and lemon peel. Cook and stir until thick and bubbly. Add cheese, cook and stir until melted (do not boil). Drain peas, return to large saucepan and add sauce. Stir to coat.
Serves 12.

FRENCH GREEN PEAS

2 (10 oz) pkgs. frozen green
  peas
8 green onions, finely chopped
1 stick butter, cut in pieces
1½ tsp. sugar
½ cup water
1 tsp. salt
½ tsp. pepper
1 medium head Boston lettuce,
  shredded

Place all ingredients, except lettuce, in large saucepan; top with lettuce. Cover pan tightly and bring to a boil. Reduce heat and simmer 10-15 minutes until peas are tender, stirring once or twice. May need to add a little water if pan seems dry.
Serves 8.

FRENCH FRIED OKRA

1½ lbs. okra
Salt and pepper to taste
1-1½ cups buttermilk
2 cups flour
2 tsp. baking powder
Oil for frying

Slice okra in ½" pieces, season with salt and pepper. Toss with buttermilk and let set 30 minutes. Mix flour and baking powder, dredge okra in this★. Fry in hot oil at least 1" deep in pan until golden brown. Drain on paper towels.
★You may want to add more salt and pepper to flour mixture; I always do as we like lots of seasoning.
Serves 4.

MACARONI CASSEROLE

8 oz pkg. elbow macaroni
1 can Cream of Mushroom soup
1 jar sliced mushrooms
  with juice
2 Tbsp. butter
¼ cup chopped green onions
¼ cup chopped onion
¼ cup chopped bell pepper
1 tsp. minced garlic
¼ cup chopped pimento
1 cup mayonnaise
3 Tbsp. melted butter
¾ lb. grated cheddar cheese
½ cup grated Monterey Jack
  cheese
1 stack Ritz crackers, crushed
½ tsp. salt
¼ tsp. pepper
⅛ tsp. cayenne

Saute green onion, onion, bell pepper and garlic in 2 tablespoons butter until tender. Add soup, mushrooms, mayonnaise, salt, pepper and cayenne. Cook and drain macaroni; add to mixture along with cheeses. Put into a casserole dish. Sprinkle cracker crumbs on top and drizzle with melted butter. Bake uncovered at 375° for 20 minutes.
Serves 8-10.

GARLIC CHEESE GRITS

4 cups water
1 cup grits
1 tsp. salt
1 stick butter
6 oz roll garlic cheese
½ tsp. garlic powder
½ tsp. pepper
1 egg, slightly beaten
1 scant cup warm milk

Boil water; add grits and salt. Continue to boil for 3 minutes. Add butter, garlic cheese, garlic powder and pepper. Boil until butter and cheese are melted. Put egg in a measuring cup and fill to 1 cup mark with warm milk. Add slowly to cheese mixture. Place in a greased casserole. Bake at 350° for 1 hour.
Serves 8-10.

Great for brunch!

GARLIC POTATOES

6 large russet potatoes
1 stick butter
Garlic salt (I prefer the kind with parsley flakes added)
Black pepper
Paprika

Peel potatoes and slice for french fries. In a greased casserole, put a layer of potatoes and dot with butter. Sprinkle heavily with garlic salt, pepper and paprika. Repeat. Bake at 350° for about 45 minutes or until tender.
Serves 6.

A favorite with steak!

HASH BROWN CASSEROLE

2 lb. pkg. frozen hash browns
½ cup chopped onion
1 tsp. minced garlic
1 Tbsp. chopped bell pepper
1 pt. sour cream
1 can Cream of Chicken soup
2 cups grated cheddar cheese
½ Tbsp. salt
½ tsp. pepper
¼ tsp. cayenne
½ cup melted butter
2 cups crushed cornflakes
¼ cup melted butter

Mix together all ingredients, except cornflakes and ¼ cup butter. Put into a greased casserole dish. Bake at 350° for 45 minutes. Remove from oven and top with cornflakes mixed with ¼ cup butter. Bake 10 more minutes.
Serves 8.

GREAT SWEET POTATOES

3 cups mashed, cooked sweet potatoes
4 Tbsp. half and half
6 Tbsp. melted margarine
1 tsp. cinnamon
¼ tsp. nutmeg
2 Tbsp. sugar
½ tsp. almond extract
⅔ cup packed brown sugar
½ cup butter
1 cup chopped toasted pecans

Combine first 7 ingredients and mix well. Put in greased casserole dish. Melt butter and brown sugar, stirring constantly, until barely melted. Pour over potatoes and top with pecans. Heat in oven or microwave until top bubbles. Can be made ahead.
Serves 6-8.

You can make a sweet potato lover out of anyone with this recipe.

SPICED SWEET POTATO FLAN

¾ cup sugar
½ tsp. salt
½ tsp. cinnamon
1 cup mashed, cooked, fresh sweet potatoes
5 large eggs, lightly beaten
1 tsp. vanilla
1½ cups evaporated milk
⅓ cup water

Caramel:
3 Tbsp. butter
⅓ cup brown sugar

Combine sugar, salt and cinnamon. Add potatoes and eggs, mix well. Stir in vanilla, milk and water, mixing all together. Melt butter in a 9" cake pan. Sprinkle brown sugar over bottom of pan. Pour in potato mixture. Place in a pan of hot water and bake at 350° for 1 hour and 15 minutes or until a knife inserted in center comes out clean. Cool and chill. To serve, run a knife around the sides and turn out on a plate.

Great holiday dish! Can be served as a dessert also, topped with whipped cream. Even people who don't like sweet potatoes love this!

CREAMY SPINACH

1 pkg. frozen chopped spinach
2 Tbsp. grated onion
2 eggs
½ cup sour cream
½ cup Parmesan cheese
½ cup grated Monterey Jack cheese
1 Tbsp. flour
2 Tbsp. butter
Salt and pepper to taste

Cook frozen spinach in a small amount of water with the onion until thawed. Beat eggs and mix with remaining ingredients; add to the spinach and onions. Bake in a greased casserole at 350° for 25-30 minutes, until center is set. Do not overcook or it will separate.
Serves 4.

WILD RICE DRESSING

2 cups cooked white rice
2 cups cooked wild rice
6 slices bacon, cooked and
  crumbled
1 onion, chopped
4 cloves garlic, minced
½ tsp. thyme
1 bay leaf
2 Tbsp. minced parsley
1 large jar sliced mushrooms
  and juice
¼-½ cup chicken broth
⅛ tsp. cayenne
Salt and pepper to taste

Saute onion and garlic in bacon drippings until soft. Add remaining ingredients, using enough broth to make a moist dressing. Season with salt and pepper. Bake at 325° for 30-40 minutes. Freezes well.
Serves 8.

Great served with smoked turkey.

SPINACH MADELAINE

1 onion, chopped
4 cloves garlic, minced
1 cup white sauce
1 roll jalapeno pepper cheese
2 pkgs. chopped spinach,
  cooked and drained
¼ cup bread crumbs
3 Tbsp. margarine
¾ tsp. celery salt
1 tsp. Worcestershire sauce
Cayenne to taste

Saute onion and garlic in margarine until clear. Add white sauce and cheese, melt together with celery salt, Worcestershire and cayenne. Add drained spinach. Put into a casserole dish and sprinkle with bread crumbs. Bake at 350° for 20 minutes.

This may be used as a vegetable dish or a hot dip. If using as a dip, use only Fritos; other chips don't work as well. Leave off bread crumbs.

CHEESY SQUASH

2-3 lbs. yellow squash
8 oz container garlic cheese
  spread
8 oz sour cream
½ tsp. salt
¼ tsp. pepper
1 small onion, chopped
2 Tbsp. butter
2 Tbsp. water

Peel and slice squash. Saute squash and onion in butter and water until tender. Mash and add cheese spread, sour cream, salt and pepper. Put in a casserole dish and bake at 350° for 20-30 minutes.
Serves 6-8.

PLANTATION SQUASH

12 medium squash
2 (10 oz) pkgs. chopped
  spinach
3 oz pkg. cream cheese
3 eggs, well beaten
6 Tbsp. melted butter
1½ Tbsp. sugar
½ tsp. seasoned salt
½ tsp. onion salt
1 Tbsp. black pepper
1 cup buttery cracker crumbs
Paprika
1 lb. bacon, cooked and
  crumbled

Wash squash and cook in boiling water. Cover and simmer 8 minutes. Drain and cool. Trim off stems. Cut squash in half lengthwise. Scoop out pulp, leaving firm shells. Mash pulp. Cook spinach and drain; add to squash pulp. Add cream cheese. Stir in eggs, butter, sugar, salts and pepper. Spoon into shells. Sprinkle with cracker crumbs, paprika and bacon. Place on greased baking sheet and cover with foil. Bake at 325° for 30 minutes.
Serves 8-10.

SQUASH CASSEROLE

4 lbs. fresh squash
1 can Cream of Chicken soup
8 oz sour cream
½ cup grated cheddar cheese
2 onions, chopped
1 pkg. Pepperidge Farm cornbread stuffing
¼ tsp. salt
¼ tsp. pepper
⅛ tsp. cayenne
1 stick margarine

Slice, boil and drain squash. Dot ½ stick margarine in large casserole; line with ½ bag stuffing. Mix squash, sour cream, soup, cheese, onion and seasonings. Pour into casserole. Top with remaining stuffing. Melt remaining margarine and drizzle over the top. Bake uncovered at 350° for 45 minutes.
Serves 10-12.

ZUCCHINI CASSEROLE I

2 onions, sliced thin
6 Tbsp. butter
2 lbs. zucchini, sliced thin
2 tomatoes, sliced thin
½ tsp. basil
Salt and pepper to taste
¼ cup grated Parmesan cheese

Saute onions in butter until wilted. Add zucchini, cook and stir 5 minutes. Add tomatoes, salt, pepper and basil. Cover and cook 5 minutes. Transfer to a casserole dish, sprinkle with cheese. Bake at 375° for 30-45 minutes.
Serves 6-8.

This may be prepared (excluding the baking) a day ahead.

ZUCCHINI CASSEROLE II

6 slices bacon
1 medium onion, coarsely
  chopped
3 large zucchini, cut in ¼"
  slices
Salt and pepper to taste
½ tsp. basil
⅛ tsp. garlic powder
½ cup Parmesan cheese

Fry bacon until crisp; remove, drain and crumble. Saute onion in bacon drippings. In a 1½ quart greased casserole, layer zucchini, seasonings, onions, bacon and cheese. Bake at 350° for 25-30 minutes.
Serves 6.

BAKED CHEDDAR TOMATOES

1½ lbs. tomatoes, peeled and
  thinly sliced
6 tsp. dry sherry
Salt and pepper to taste
12 Tbsp. heavy cream
18 Tbsp. grated cheddar
  cheese
Minced parsley

Divide tomato slices among 6 buttered 4" gratin dishes. Add 1 teaspoon sherry to each dish. Sprinkle with salt and pepper. Bake at 300° for 20-30 minutes until soft. Add to each dish 2 tablespoons cream and 3 tablespoons grated cheese. Bake for 15 minutes more. Garnish with minced parsley.
Serves 6.

Best in the summer when tomatoes are at their peak. Can also be done as a casserole.

VEGETABLE CASSEROLE

1 bunch fresh broccoli
6 new potatoes, halved
6 small yellow squash, halved
8-10 tiny whole onions
3-4 carrots, cut in fourths
1½ cups cauliflower florets
1 can Cream of Mushroom soup
1 roll of garlic or jalapeno
  cheese
½ tsp. salt
¼ tsp. pepper
⅛ tsp. cayenne
½ tsp. garlic powder
Milk to thin sauce

Boil or steam vegetables until half done. Transfer to a large casserole dish. In a saucepan, melt cheese with soup over medium heat. Add seasonings and milk to thin. Pour over vegetables. Bake at 350° for 20-30 minutes until tender.
Serves 8-10.

You may use all of the above vegetables or a combination of any.

This is a beautiful dish if you take the time to try and arrange the vegetables according to colors. Susan gave me this idea.

RATATOUILLE
(Microwave)

1 medium onion, sliced
1 medium green pepper, cut into strips
1 medium eggplant, peeled and cut into ½" slices
1 clove garlic, minced or pressed
¼ cup olive or vegetable oil
2 medium zucchini, cut into ¼" slices
2 tsp. parsley flakes
1 tsp. basil leaves
1 tsp. salt
½ tsp. sugar
⅛ tsp. black pepper
3 medium tomatoes, peeled and cut into wedges

In a 3 quart casserole, combine onion, green pepper, eggplant, garlic and oil. Cover. Microwave at high for 4-6 minutes, or until onion is tender and eggplant is translucent.

Stir in remaining ingredients, except tomatoes. Cover. Microwave at high for 5-7 minutes, or until vegetables are almost tender, stirring after half the cooking time.

Gently mix in tomatoes. Cover. Microwave at high 2 minutes, or until tomatoes are heated and vegetables are tender, stirring after half the cooking time.

Serves 6.

This is one of the few ways Ed will eat eggplant. Very tasty.

The only safe and sure way to destroy an enemy is to make him your friend.

Meat

S.O.S.
(Creamed Beef on Toast)

1½-2 lbs. ground chuck
1 large onion, chopped
3-4 cloves garlic, minced
2-3 cups milk (I use half milk
  and half and half)
2-3 boiled eggs, chopped
2 Tbsp. cornstarch
Salt and pepper to taste

Saute meat with onion and garlic until browned. Salt and pepper to taste. Add enough milk to completely cover the meat mixture. Simmer about 10-15 minutes. Add eggs and simmer a few more minutes. Mix cornstarch with a little milk and add to mixture to thicken. Serve over toast.
Serves 4-6.

A great breakfast! My mother always makes this for her grandsons when we go home. As much as I've made it, they always say Grandma's is better.

HEARTY MEXICAN CORNBREAD

1 cup cornmeal, plain
2 eggs, beaten
1 cup milk
½ tsp. soda
¾ tsp. salt
1 small can cream-style corn
¼ cup bacon drippings
½ lb. ground meat
1 large onion, chopped
½ lb. grated cheddar cheese
2 jalapeno peppers, seeded
  and chopped

Mix together the cornmeal, eggs, milk, soda, salt, corn and bacon drippings. Set aside. Saute the meat and onions until done. Pour half the batter in a large greased and heated iron skillet. Sprinkle the grated cheese on top, then the meat and onion mixture. Sprinkle with the peppers and pour the remaining batter over all. Bake at 350° for 45-50 minutes.
Serves 4-6.

A meal in itself!

Do not judge your friend
until you stand in his place.

MEXICAN DINNER

2 (16 oz) cans refried beans
  (I like jalapeno)
1½-2 lbs. ground beef
1 pkg. taco seasoning
1 onion, chopped
1 lb. grated cheddar cheese
1-1½ cups guacamole
8 oz sour cream
1 small can chopped black
  olives
6 green onions, chopped
2 tomatoes, chopped
8 oz picante sauce

Tortilla chips
Warm flour tortillas

Brown meat and onions, drain. Add taco seasoning and follow package directions. Butter a 9x13 pan, place beans in pan, then meat mixture. Cover with picante sauce and top with cheese. Bake covered at 350° for 15 minutes. Uncover and bake an additional 15 minutes. Remove from oven and top with guacamole, sour cream, green onions, tomatoes and olives. Serve with chips to dip into or spoon onto warm tortillas.
Serves 8.

A great casual dinner!

SPAGHETTI AND BEEF CASSEROLE

2 lbs. ground beef
2 medium onions, chopped
Large jar sliced mushrooms
2 (8 oz) cans tomato sauce
6 oz can tomato paste
1½ tsp. oregano
1 tsp. garlic powder
½ tsp. basil
Salt and pepper to taste
2 (7 oz) pkgs. spaghetti
8 oz pkg. cream cheese
2 cups cottage cheese
6-8 green onions, chopped
½ cup sour cream
½ cup Parmesan cheese,
  grated

Brown ground beef and onions and saute until meat is browned and onions tender. Drain well.
Combine mushrooms, tomato sauce, tomato paste, oregano, garlic powder, basil, salt and pepper; add to meat mixture, mixing well. Simmer uncovered 15 minutes.
Cook spaghetti as usual, drain. Place half of spaghetti in a large buttered baking dish.
★ Combine cream cheese, cottage cheese, green onions and sour cream. Mix well. Spoon cream cheese mixture over spaghetti layer, spreading evenly.
Place remaining spaghetti over cream cheese mixture. Pour meat sauce over spaghetti and sprinkle with Parmesan cheese. Bake at 350° for 30 minutes. May freeze.
Serves 12.

★ I usually add more oregano and basil to cream cheese mixture, as we like things spicy.

SPAGHETTI PIE - MICROWAVE

½ (10 oz) pkg. vermicelli,
  cooked
2 Tbsp. butter
½ cup grated Parmesan cheese
2 eggs, well beaten
1 lb. ground chuck
½ cup chopped onion
¼ cup chopped green pepper
1 (8 oz) can stewed tomatoes,
  undrained
1 (6 oz) can tomato paste
1 tsp. sugar
¾ tsp. oregano
1 tsp. salt and pepper
½ tsp. garlic powder
1 cup cream style cottage
  cheese
½ cup (2 oz) shredded mozzarella cheese
12 pepperoni slices
4 tsp. fresh parsley, optional

Stir butter and Parmesan cheese into hot vermicelli. Add eggs - stir well. Shape with spoon in 10" pie plate. Microwave on high 3 minutes or until set. Crumble beef in 2 quart casserole - stir in onion and pepper. Cover and microwave on high 5-6 minutes - stir at 2 minute intervals - drain. Stir in tomatoes, paste and seasonings. Cover - microwave on high 3½-4 minutes, stirring once. Spread cottage cheese evenly over pie shell. Top with meat sauce -cover with plastic wrap and microwave on high 6-6½ minutes and sprinkle with mozzarella cheese. Microwave uncovered on high 30 seconds until cheese begins to melt. Garnish with pepperoni and parsley. Microwave uncovered on high 1 minute. Let stand 10 minutes before serving. Makes 1 pie.

Meat sauce could be done on top of the stove to save time.

This is a favorite. I make two at a time. Great for taking to a sick friend. My friend, Lin, brought it to me after I had foot surgery. A tossed salad, french bread and spaghetti pie; ideal for a perfect meal!

 All people smile in the same language.

SAM'S MEATBALLS AND SPAGHETTI

Sauce:
Cooking oil (for roux)
Flour (for roux)
1 large onion, finely chopped
4 (8 oz) cans tomato sauce
4 cans water
Salt, pepper to taste
1 bunch parsley, finely chopped
2 bunches green onions, divided, finely chopped
2 tsp. Worcestershire sauce
1½ tsp. garlic powder
2 Tbsp. ketchup
1½ Tbsp. bar-b-cue sauce
1 large bell pepper, cut in 6 pieces
1½ tsp. basil
1½ tsp. oregano

Meatballs:
3 lbs. ground chuck
3 eggs

In a 5 quart black iron pot, pour just enough oil to cover bottom of pot - add ⅓ to ½ cup flour and mix well. Cook over medium heat, stirring constantly, until golden brown. Turn heat to low - add onion - stir, cover and cook about 5 minutes, stirring once or twice. Turn heat back up to medium high - add tomato sauce, water, salt, pepper, ½ of the parsley, 1 bunch green onions, Worcestershire, garlic, ketchup, bar-b-que sauce, bell pepper, basil and oregano. Bring to boil - turn heat to low and cook 30 minutes, stirring often.

Meanwhile, make meatballs. Combine ground chuck, eggs, remainder of parsley, green onions, salt and pepper to taste. Form into 1" meatballs and drop into sauce. Cook, stirring often, for another 30 minutes. Serve over spaghetti. Sprinkle with Parmesan cheese. Serves 6-8.

My husband, Sam, is an excellent cook. Sam's grandma taught him the basic sauce and Sam added his own touches. This was also one of my daddy's favorites, and he always made sure he ended up with any leftover meatballs and sauce.

Friendship is the only cement that will ever hold the world together.

ITALIAN SPAGHETTI AND MEATBALLS

**2 slices French bread, torn in
small pieces
½ cup milk
1 egg, slightly beaten
1 lb. ground chuck, ground
twice
¼ lb. Italian sausage, remove
from casing
6 Tbsp. freshly grated
Parmesan cheese
2 Tbsp. chopped parsley
1 Tbsp. olive oil
2 tsp. minced garlic
1 tsp. grated lemon peel
¼ tsp. ground allspice
1 tsp. salt
¼ tsp. pepper
¼ cup oil
Tomato sauce (recipe follows)**

Soak bread in milk for 5 minutes. Squeeze dry and discard milk. In a large bowl, combine bread, egg, beef, sausage, cheese, parsley, olive oil, garlic, peel and spices. Knead mixture until well blended and fluffy. Shape into 1-1½" balls. Cover and chill 1 hour.
Heat oil in skillet and fry meatballs 5 or 6 at a time, shaking pan. Drain.
Serves 4-6.

ITALIAN TOMATO SAUCE

**4 Tbsp. olive oil
2 cans Progresso whole peeled
tomatoes
1 cup finely chopped onion
6 Tbsp. tomato paste
2 tsp. dried basil
1 Tbsp. sugar
1 tsp. salt
½ tsp. pepper
4-5 cloves garlic, minced
4 Tbsp. burgundy**

Saute onion and garlic in oil. Add remaining ingredients and simmer on low 1½ hours. If it seems too thick, add tomato juice; you should never add water!
Press through a seive or put in food processor. Put back into pot and add meatballs. Simmer together at least one hour.
Cook spaghetti. Butter a large bowl and add spaghetti. Sprinkle with freshly grated Parmesan cheese. Pour meatballs and sauce over.

A very unique flavor!

BEEF ENCHILADA CASSEROLE

2 lbs. ground meat
1 onion, chopped
2 Tbsp. chili powder
2 (4 oz) cans green chiles
2 cans Cream of Mushroom
   soup
10 oz can enchilada sauce
1 pkg. tortillas
½ lb. cheddar cheese, grated
½ lb. Monterey Jack cheese,
   grated

Brown meat, add onion and chili powder. Add chiles, soup and enchilada sauce. Tear tortillas in pieces and line a 9x13 pan with half. Pour ½ of mixture over tortilla pieces, remaining tortillas and sauce. Top with grated cheese. Bake at 375° for 45 minutes. This can be made ahead and refrigerated.
Serves 6.

My Aunt Loreta is a marvelous cook. This is only one of her "delicious and easy" recipes. There are quite a few in the cookbook.

LASAGNA

1 lb. ground pork
2 lbs. ground chuck
1 cup chopped onion
1 Tbsp. minced garlic
2 Tbsp. minced carrot
2 Tbsp. olive oil
1 lb. 12 oz can tomatoes
2 (8 oz) cans tomato sauce
1½ Tbsp. parsley flakes
1 cup Chianti
1 Tbsp. sugar
Salt, pepper to taste
1 tsp. basil
1 tsp. crushed oregano
Lasagna noodles
2 (1 lb.) cartons cottage cheese
½ cup Parmesan cheese
1 Tbsp. parsley flakes
1 tsp. salt
2 eggs, beaten
1 tsp. oregano
18 oz grated mozzarella cheese

Brown meat, onion, garlic and carrot in olive oil. Drain off fat. Break tomatoes up with a fork and add to meat mixture with tomato sauce, 1½ tablespoons parsley, sugar, 1 teaspoon each basil and oregano. Salt and pepper to taste. Add Chianti, simmer uncovered 1 hour or until thickened. Cook and drain noodles. Mix cottage cheese, Parmesan cheese, 1 tablespoon parsley, 1 teaspoon salt, eggs and 1 teaspoon oregano. In a 9x13 pan, layer half the noodles, sauce, ½ mozzarella and ½ cottage cheese mixture. Repeat, reserving enough sauce for a thin layer on top. Spread sauce over top and sprinkle with Parmesan and mozzarella, if any is left. Bake uncovered at 350° for 45 minutes. Let stand 15 minutes before cutting. Freezes well.
Serves 12.

CHUCK WAGON

2 onions, chopped
½ bell pepper, chopped
1½ tsp. minced garlic
3 ribs celery, chopped
½ tsp. oregano
½ tsp. basil
1¼ tsp. salt
1 tsp. pepper
2-3 Tbsp. olive oil
Few drops Worcestershire
  sauce
2 tsp. parsley flakes
6 oz can tomato paste
Large can Italian tomatoes
3 lbs. ground beef
8 oz pkg. wide egg noodles
2 lbs. sharp cheddar cheese,
  grated
1 small can black olives,
  chopped

Brown vegetables in olive oil. Add seasonings, tomatoes (chopped), tomato paste and beef. Simmer 2-3 hours. Cook noodles as usual and drain. Layer noodles, olives, cheese and sauce. Save some cheese to sprinkle on top. Bake at 350° for about 20 minutes.
Freeze leftovers in muffin tins for individual servings.
Serves 8-10.

CABBAGE ROLLS

9-10 cups flour
¼ cup shortening or oil
¼ cup sugar
2 Tbsp. salt
3½ cups half water and milk
2 pkgs. yeast
½ tsp. sugar
½ cup warm water
1 head cabbage, grated
4 onions, chopped
2 Tbsp. bacon grease
2 lbs. ground meat
Salt, pepper

Dissolve yeast and ½ teaspoon sugar in ½ cup warm water, set aside. In a bowl, mix shortening or oil, ¼ cup sugar and salt. Add milk and water mixture, mix well. Then add yeast mixture. Add approximately 9-10 cups flour, dough will be sticky. Let rise until double (1-1½ hours), work down and let rise again (½ hour). Work down and divide into 24 balls. Cook cabbage and onions in bacon grease. Brown meat with salt and pepper to taste, mix with cabbage. Roll each dough ball into a circle and spoon filling in center. Fold over and pinch edges. Bake at 400° on greased cookie sheets for 20 minutes. Makes 24.

My family stands around and eats them as they come out of the oven. Worth the effort!

HELEN'S MEAT LOAF

1½ lbs. ground round
1 egg, beaten
1½ cups soft bread crumbs
½ cup ketchup or small can
  tomato sauce
1½ tsp. Worcestershire sauce
1 onion, finely chopped
¼ cup chopped parsley
Salt and pepper to taste
¼ tsp. oregano
¼ tsp. tarragon
¼ tsp. basil
¼ tsp. marjoram
4 slices American cheese
1 can Hunts Herb tomato sauce

Mix all ingredients together except cheese and Herb tomato sauce. Divide into two equal parts. Mold 1 part and put 2 slices of cheese on top. Mold second part and place on top of cheese. Mold into a loaf and put in a baking dish. Put 2 slices of cheese on top, pour Herb tomato sauce over it. Bake at 350°, covered, for one hour. Uncover and bake 20-30 minutes longer. Serves 4-6.

My kids love Grandma's meat loaf almost as much as I do. Thanks Mom!

TWO CRUST PIZZA

2 loaves frozen bread dough
1 lb. ground meat
1 medium onion, chopped
1 medium bell pepper, chopped
6 oz can sliced mushrooms,
  drained
2 Tbsp. cornmeal
1 cup grated Parmesan cheese
8 oz sliced mozzarella cheese
15 oz jar extra thick spaghetti
  sauce
2 tsp. thyme
1 tsp. crushed fennel
Milk
Cornmeal

Thaw bread, make each loaf into a ball. Cover, let rise until nearly double. Punch down, let rest 10 minutes. Meanwhile, cook ground meat, onion and pepper until done. Drain well. On floured surface, roll ½ dough into a 13" circle. Grease 12" pizza pan, sprinkle with 2 table-spoons cornmeal, fit dough into pan. Sprinkle with ½ cup Parmesan cheese. Top with meat mixture, mushrooms and cheese slices. Spoon spaghetti sauce over this, sprinkle with thyme, fennel and remaining Parmesan cheese. Roll rest of dough to 13" circle, place over filling. Fold extra dough under bottom crust, pinching to seal. Cut slits in top to let steam escape. Bake at 400° for 15 minutes. Brush milk on top and sprinkle with cornmeal. Bake 15 minutes more, until nice and brown. Let set 10-15 minutes before cutting. Cut in wedges. Serves 6-8.

Aunt Loreta does it again!

CHILI

2 medium onions, chopped
1 cup chopped bell pepper
6 cloves garlic, minced
2 lbs. lean ground beef
4 Tbsp. chili powder
2 tsp. ground cumin
3 tsp. oregano
1 Tbsp. salt
½ tsp. pepper
1 Tbsp. oil
2 (1 lb.) cans kidney beans
4 cups tomatoes and liquid

Brown vegetables with meat and seasonings in oil until done. Add beans and tomatoes. Cover. Simmer 3 hours.
Serves 4-6.

CHILI BEANS

1 lb. hot bulk sausage
1½ lbs. ground beef
1 onion, chopped
½ cup brown sugar
½ cup Worcestershire sauce
1 Tbsp. chili powder
1 large can Ranch Style beans
1 can navy beans
1 can kidney beans
1 can pork and beans
1 can jalapeno beans
1 (16 oz) bottle hickory
  bar-b-que sauce

Saute sausage and beef with onions until done. Drain. Add remaining ingredients and simmer about an hour.
Serve over hot dogs or have a "Chili Throw On" dinner:
  Serve rice, chips, onions, grated cheese, chopped jalapenos, chopped tomatoes, chopped lettuce, etc. Pile the chili beans on top of rice and chips and add whatever else you desire.
Serves 12.

Enjoy!

DEER CHILI

1 lb. bacon, cut in pieces and
   brown to a crisp
★ 3 lbs. ground venison
Dash sugar
2 Tbsp. chili powder
1½ tsp. pepper
1′Tbsp. salt
1 tsp. comino seed
2 tsp. garlic powder
4 onions, chopped
4 #303 cans tomatoes (I use
   stewed)
4 (1 lb.) cans kidney beans
Water

Brown bacon to a crisp and add venison; brown. Add remaining ingredients and enough water to cover all. Simmer about an hour. Good served over rice, top with grated cheese and chopped jalapenos.
Serves 8-10.

★ When I run out of venison, I use ground chuck. Bacon really adds a good flavor to chili!

HUNGARIAN SCHRAZY

1 lb. round steak, cut in 4
   pieces
1 medium onion, chopped
½ cup chopped bell pepper
¾ cup grated carrot
⅛ lb. salt pork, chopped
Salt and pepper
1 cup boiling water

Pound flour into steak, season. Combine remaining ingredients except water. Place small amount of mixture on each piece of steak. Roll, tie securely. Brown in hot oil. Add water. Cover and simmer 1½ hours. Thicken stock for gravy.
Serves 4.

TERIYAKI

4 lbs. chuck steaks, cut very
   thin
1 large bottle soy sauce
½ tsp. ginger
¼ cup brown sugar
½ lemon, squeezed
Garlic salt

Mix together the soy sauce, same amount of water, ginger, brown sugar and lemon juice. Pour over chuck steaks. Cover generously with garlic salt. Cover and refrigerate 24 hours. Turn frequently. Grill over hot coals.
Serves 8.

GRILLADES

2 round steaks (½" thick)
3 Tbsp. vegetable oil
1 Tbsp. flour
1 cup chopped onion
1 clove garlic, minced
2 bell peppers, chopped
1½ cups peeled, chopped
  tomatoes
½ cup water
2 Tbsp. chopped parsley
½ tsp. thyme
1 tsp. salt
¼ tsp. pepper
1 bay leaf

Cut each steak into 4 pieces. Brown well in hot oil, remove. Add flour to oil, cook until golden brown. Add onion, garlic and bell pepper, cook until soft. Add remaining ingredients and meat. Cover, simmer over low heat 1½-2 hours. Check occasionally. If it sticks or gravy gets too thick, add a little hot water. Serve with rice. Serves 8.

HUNGARIAN GOULASH

¼ cup flour
1 tsp. salt
¼ tsp. pepper
2 tsp. paprika
3 lbs. lean chuck or round
  steak, cut in 1¼" cubes
3 Tbsp. oil
1½ cups chopped onion
1 garlic clove, minced
10½ oz can beef broth
½ cup water
2 (1 lb.) cans tomatoes
½ tsp. salt
¼ tsp. pepper
2 bay leaves
2 tsp. caraway seeds
½ cup water
1 cup sour cream
1½ pkgs. (12 oz) medium
  noodles, cooked
¼ cup butter, melted

Combine flour, 1 teaspoon salt, ¼ teaspoon pepper and paprika in bag; add meat. Shake to coat well. Reserve flour mixture. Heat oil in heavy dutch oven and brown meat on all sides. Remove. Saute onion and garlic in drippings. Add meat, broth, ½ cup water, tomatoes, ½ teaspoon salt, ¼ teaspoon pepper, bay leaves and caraway seeds. Cover, simmer 2 hours, stir occasionally. Remove bay leaves. Blend 3 tablespoons reserved flour and ½ cup water, add to pan. Stir constantly on low until thickened. Stir in sour cream and heat (do not boil). Toss noodles with butter and serve with goulash. Serves 6.

ITALIAN STUFFED STEAK

2-3 lbs. top round steak, cut in
  serving pieces
3 cups Italian bread crumbs
¼ cup grated Parmesan cheese
¼ cup grated Romano cheese
2 raw eggs
2 boiled eggs, grated
1 onion, chopped
½ bell pepper, chopped
1½ tsp. minced garlic
3 Tbsp. chopped parsley
¾ tsp. salt
½ tsp. pepper
¾ tsp. Italian seasoning

Sauce:
Large jar Ragu sauce
¼ cup chopped onion
3 cloves garlic, minced
1 Tbsp. olive oil
Salt, pepper to taste

Pound steak with meat mallet until thin. Combine bread crumbs, cheeses, boiled eggs and parsley. Mix well. In blender, combine raw eggs, onion, bell pepper and garlic. Blend until pureed. Add to bread crumb mixture with seasonings. Spread steak with mixture and roll up. Secure with a toothpick or tie with string. In a sauce pan, saute ¼ cup onion and garlic in olive oil until clear. Add Ragu, salt and pepper. Simmer 15 minutes.

Put meat rolls in a casserole dish and cover with sauce. Bake at 325° for 3-4 hours.
Serves 6-8.

CHINESE FLANK STEAK

1 (1½ lb.) flank steak
2 Tbsp. soy sauce
1 tsp. Worcestershire sauce
Dash Tabasco
3 Tbsp. oil
1 medium onion, sliced
½ bell pepper, in strips
2 cloves garlic, minced
4 oz jar sliced mushrooms
2 Tbsp. cornstarch
1½ cups beef broth

Slice steak very thin diagonally. Place in bowl. Sprinkle with soy sauce, Worcestershire and Tabasco. Toss to mix well. Heat oil in skillet, add seasoned meat. Cook quickly, stirring constantly, until it loses its pink color. Remove with slotted spoon. Stir onion, pepper, and garlic into drippings. Saute until soft. Stir in mushrooms and liquid. Blend cornstarch into broth in small bowl until smooth and stir into vegetables. Cook, stirring, until sauce thickens and boils 3 minutes. Return meat to mixture and heat.
Serve over rice.
Serves 4.

PORK CHOPS IN WINE

4 (½") center cut chops
2 Tbsp. butter
1 small onion, chopped
1 Tbsp. flour
½ cup white wine
¼ cup beef broth
1 tsp. Dijon mustard
Salt and freshly ground black
  pepper

Brown chops in butter over medium heat for 15-20 minutes on each side. Remove chops, add onion and brown slowly. Blend in flour; add wine and broth, stirring constantly, until thickened. Return chops to sauce and simmer 10 minutes. Add mustard, salt and pepper to taste.
Serves 4.

Good served with buttered noodles.

SANDRA'S PORK ENCHILADAS

4-6 lb. boston butt pork
  roast
1 (16 oz) can Hunt's tomatoes
2 (8 oz) cans tomato sauce
Juice of 2 lemons
2 Tbsp. oil
1 cup chopped green onions
½ cup chopped parsley
4-5 cloves garlic, minced
¼ cup chopped bell pepper
1 tsp. salt
½ tsp. pepper
¼ tsp. chili powder
Dash cumin
2 cups grated cheddar cheese
2 pkgs. corn tortillas

Boil roast and shred meat. Saute onion, garlic and pepper in oil. Add tomatoes, which have been cut up fine, tomato sauce, lemon juice and seasonings. Simmer about 20 minutes. Combine meat with half of sauce mixture. Lightly fry tortillas in a little oil to soften. Fill with meat mixture and roll up. Lay seam side down in a casserole dish. Pour remaining sauce over and sprinkle with cheese. Bake at 350° for 20-30 minutes.
For variation try a 3-5 lb. chicken. Boil and shred just like the pork roast.
Serves 8.

Sandra has learned her Spanish and French cooking from a dear lady whom we all deeply miss - Mrs. Hijuelos. This is only one of her superb recipes.

FETUCCINI MILANO

★ **1 lb. Italian sausage**
3 cups sliced, fresh mushrooms
1½ tsp. minced garlic
1 bell pepper, chopped
1 cup chopped parsley
1 cup chopped green onions
1 tsp. basil, crumbled
½ tsp. oregano
¼ tsp. rosemary
½ tsp. pepper
¾ tsp. salt
½ cup olive oil
½ cup butter
Cooked pkg. fetuccini
**Freshly grated Parmesan
  cheese**

Brown sausage, remove from skillet and drain on paper towels. Saute mushrooms, garlic, bell pepper, onion, parsley and seasonings in oil and butter until vegetables are soft. Remove from heat; stir in sausage. Toss with hot fetuccini. Sprinkle generously with Parmesan cheese. Serve immediately.
Serves 4.

★ Remove sausage from casing.

I sent this recipe to an Italian Restaurant in Shreveport and won dinner for two - they had my name on their menu for a month.

CITY CHICKEN

**1 lb. veal (I cut the meat from
  chops)**
1 lb. pork (boneless pork chops)
1 lb. beef (sirloin)
2 eggs
¾ cup milk
¾-1 cup flour
½ tsp. salt
**¼ tsp. pepper (I prefer seasoned
  pepper)**
1 onion, chopped
3-4 cloves garlic, minced
Small wooden skewers

Beat the two eggs with milk. Mix flour with the salt and pepper. Cut the meat into cubes and alternate on skewers. Dip into the egg-milk mixture and then roll in flour mixture. Brown in a little oil on the stove. Put in a roaster and sprinkle with onions and garlic. Pour 2 cups of water over and bake at 350° for 40 minutes - 1 hour. I usually sprinkle more salt and pepper over before I bake it.
Serves 4-6.

*We don't know why it's called City Chicken. For as long as I can remember it's what I wanted mother to make for my birthday dinner.
A very special dish from a very special lady!*

Mothers, as well as fools, sometimes walk
where angels fear to tread.

Poultry

BAKED CHICKEN BREASTS

6 chicken breasts
1 cup sour cream
2 Tbsp. lemon juice
2 tsp. Worcestershire sauce
1 tsp. celery salt
1 tsp. onion salt
1 tsp. parsley flakes
3-4 cloves garlic, minced
1 tsp. paprika
2 tsp. salt
½ tsp. pepper
1 cup dry bread crumbs
½ cup margarine

Combine sour cream with lemon juice, Worcestershire and seasonings. Add chicken and coat well. Cover and place in refrigerator for 8-12 hours. Remove chicken and roll in bread crumbs. Place in a shallow baking dish. Melt margarine and pour ½ over the chicken. Bake uncovered at 350° for 45 minutes. Pour remaining butter over chicken and bake 10-15 minutes more.
Serves 6.

ELEGANTE' CHICKEN

4 boned and skinned chicken breasts
½ cup flour mixed with salt, pepper, garlic salt
½ stick butter
3 tsp. brandy
2 tsp. minced green onions
1 tsp. minced garlic
¼ lb. sliced fresh mushrooms
½ cup half and half
2 Tbsp. dijon mustard
2 tsp. minced parsley
Salt, pepper to taste

Dredge chicken in flour mixture. Saute in butter until done. Add brandy and ignite, shake until flames die out. Arrange chicken on a platter and keep warm.
In same pan, saute green onions and garlic for 1 minute; add mushrooms and saute 3 minutes. Add cream, reduce heat and stir until thickened. Stir in mustard, parsley, salt and pepper. Pour over chicken.
Serves 4.

Good with rice pilaf.

PARMESAN CHICKEN

1 cup bread crumbs
⅓ cup Parmesan cheese
¼ tsp. ground oregano
¼ tsp. pepper
¼ tsp. salt
¼ tsp. garlic salt
2 cloves garlic, minced
¾ cup melted margarine
4-6 pieces of chicken

Combine bread crumbs, cheese and seasonings. Set aside. Saute minced garlic in margarine. Dip chicken in margarine, then bread crumb mixture. Place on baking dish. Sprinkle with remaining crumbs and drizzle with the leftover margarine. Bake at 350° for 55 minutes.
Serves 4-6.

LEMON CHICKEN WITH BROCCOLI

3-4 chicken breasts, boned and
  cut in bite size pieces
1-2 lemons, sliced thin
1 bunch broccoli, steamed
Oil for frying

Marinade:
½ tsp.salt
1 Tbsp. sherry
1 Tbsp. soy sauce
½ tsp. sugar

Batter:
2 eggs
¼ cup cornstarch
½ tsp. baking powder

Sauce:
1 Tbsp. oil
1 tsp. salt
3 Tbsp. sugar
1 Tbsp. cornstarch
2 Tbsp. lemon juice
1 cup chicken broth

Marinate chicken for 15-30 minutes in marinade mixture.
Beat eggs for batter, add cornstarch and baking powder. Remove chicken from marinade and coat with batter. Fry in hot oil until golden brown.
Heat oil for sauce, slowly add remaining ingredients. Cook over medium heat until thick and clear.
Arrange broccoli on a platter. Put chicken on top of broccoli; pour sauce over all.
Garnish with lemon slices. Serve immediately. Serves 4-6.

CHICKEN VERMOUTH

½ cup dry vermouth
¾ cup chopped green onions
Dash thyme
4 boned and skinned chicken
  breasts
2 cans Cream of Mushroom
  soup
½ cup flour
½ tsp. salt
¼ tsp. pepper
⅛ tsp. paprika
Dash cayenne
½ lb. sliced fresh mushrooms
½ cup butter
1 egg beaten in ½ cup milk

Mix flour and seasonings. Cut chicken into bite size pieces. Dip chicken in egg mixture and coat with flour mixture. Brown chicken in butter in skillet, then put into a casserole dish. Saute fresh mushrooms in butter until tender, add to chicken. Combine remaining ingredients and pour over chicken. Bake at 350° for 45 minutes.
Serves 4-6.

STEWED CHICKEN AND GERMAN DUMPLINGS

1 (3½-4 lb.) chicken
½ cup cooking oil
½ cup flour
1 large onion, finely chopped
1 bell pepper, cut in 6 pieces
2 tsp. garlic powder
Salt and pepper to taste
1 bunch green onions,
  finely chopped
1½ tsp. basil
1 tsp. Worcestershire sauce
3 (8 oz) cans tomato sauce
3 tomato sauce cans of chicken
  broth

Dumplings:
4 cups Bisquick
1⅓ cups chicken broth
½ cup chopped fresh parsley
½ tsp. salt
¼ tsp. pepper

Cook chicken in enough water to cover until tender. Remove chicken and save broth. Debone chicken and cut in chunks. In a 4 quart black iron pot, heat oil (medium heat) and flour. Cook, stirring constantly, until golden brown. Reduce heat to low and add onion. Cover and cook about 5 minutes until onion is wilted, stirring a couple of times. Return heat to medium and add seasonings, tomato sauce and broth. Bring to a boil, stirring often. Reduce heat and simmer 30 minutes. Mix dumplings and let set. After sauce has cooked 30 minutes, add chicken (if sauce is too thick, add a little broth) and cook 30-45 minutes longer. Cook dumplings while sauce is cooking.

You will probably need to cook the dumplings in 3 batches. If your pan is large enough, you may get by with 2 batches. The dumpling dough will be sticky. Use remaining broth (water if needed) to cook the dumplings. Bring broth to boil and drop dough by large spoonfuls on to broth. Cook uncovered over low heat 10 minutes; cover and cook 10 minutes. Remove to platter and keep warm. Cook next batch, adding more liquid if necessary. Serve sauce over dumplings. Green peas are very pretty with this.

Serves 6-8. (20-24 dumplings)

One of Sam's favorites.

Trouble is a sieve through which we sift our acquaintances. Those who are too big to pass through are our friends.

CHICKEN ENCHILADAS

1 chicken, boiled and deboned
Chicken broth (from chicken)
1 can Cream of Mushroom soup
8 oz sour cream
4 chopped green onions
Small can Rotel tomatoes,
  chopped
1 lb. cheddar cheese, grated
★ 1 pkg. corn tortillas
Salt and pepper to taste

Combine chicken, soup, sour cream, green onions, drained Rotel tomatoes and enough broth to mix well.
Put a small scoop of mixture on each tortilla and roll up. Place seam side down in a baking dish. Pour leftover sauce over all and top with cheese.
Cover with foil and bake at 350° for 30 minutes.
Serves 6.

★ You need to soften in a little oil. This is also good if you use flour tortillas. Can use half cheddar and half Monterey Jack cheese, also.
Serves 6.

CHICKEN ITALIAN

2 (4 lb.) hens
½ cup butter
2 bell peppers, chopped
2 Tbsp. chili powder
3 (8 oz) cans tomato sauce
2 pkgs. frozen lima beans,
  peas or corn
5 onions, chopped
1 cup ripe olives, sliced
2 cans mushrooms
1 can stewed tomatoes
2 tsp. garlic powder
3 ribs celery, chopped
1½ tsp. oregano
1½ tsp. basil
1 lb. grated cheddar cheese
Worcestershire sauce, salt
  and pepper to taste
16 oz pkg. thin spaghetti

Cook chickens whole with celery tops and 2 onions. Allow chickens to cool in broth. Skim off fat. Reserve broth for cooking spaghetti. Remove meat from bones. Saute 3 chopped onions in butter; add bell pepper, chili powder, tomato sauce, beans, olives, mushrooms, tomatoes, garlic, celery, basil and oregano. Mix with cooked spaghetti (which has been cooked in broth), adding Worcestershire, salt and pepper to taste. Divide into 2 casseroles, arranging chicken through spaghetti. Sprinkle grated cheese on top and heat in oven at 350° for 30-40 minutes. Freezes well.
Serves 16-20.

CHICKEN TETRAZZINI

2 cans button mushrooms
6 ribs celery, chopped
1 large onion, chopped
4 Tbsp. butter
1 pt. chicken broth
2 tsp. garlic, minced
1 can Cream of Mushroom soup
½ cup grated cheese
1 pkg. spaghetti, cooked and
  drained
4 cups cooked chicken, cut in
  bite size pieces
1 cup chopped pecans
Salt and pepper to taste
½ cup sherry or white wine
★ Parmesan cheese

Cook celery, onions and garlic in butter until tender. Add mushrooms and broth and simmer 15 minutes. Slowly add soup, then cheese and spaghetti; bring to a boil, then let stand 1 hour. Add chicken, ½ cup nuts, salt and pepper. Stir slowly and add wine or sherry. Turn into a large casserole, sprinkle with the remaining nuts and heat thoroughly in a 350° oven, about 30 minutes. Do not allow to bubble.
Serves 10-12.

★ Parmesan can be sprinkled on top also. Gives a nice touch!

DOROTHY'S CHICKEN SPAGHETTI

1 chicken, boiled and deboned
Chicken broth
1 bell pepper, chopped
4 cloves garlic, minced
1 onion, chopped
3 ribs celery, chopped
1 stick margarine
1 large can tomato sauce
1 small pkg. spaghetti
Salt, pepper to taste
Parmesan cheese or ½ cup
  grated cheddar cheese

Boil and debone chicken, save broth. Saute pepper, onion, garlic and celery in butter until tender. Add tomato sauce and simmer about 30 minutes. Cook spaghetti as directed and drain. Mix spaghetti, chicken and sauce together; add broth to moisten as needed. Salt and pepper to taste. Serve with Parmesan cheese or grated cheddar cheese.
Serves 4-6.

Dorothy's claim to fame is not cooking, but this shows me it could be!

Friends are made by many acts -
and lost by only one.

MILLER'S SPANISH GUMBO

3-4 lb. chicken
2 (7 oz) pkgs. yellow rice
1 bell pepper, chopped
2 onions, chopped
3-4 ribs celery, chopped
4-6 green onions, chopped
5-6 cloves garlic, minced
1 pt. oysters
1½ lbs. boiled shrimp, boiled
  with lots of seasoning and
  crab boil
1 can asparagus spears
1 (10 oz) pkg. frozen peas
1 jar whole pimento
2 tsp. salt
2 tsp. parsley flakes
1 tsp. poultry seasoning
1½ tsp. black pepper
½-1 tsp. cayenne
1 Tbsp. crab boil liquid,
  for chicken

Boil the chicken with crab boil and sprinkle with salt, pepper and garlic salt. Cook rice according to package directions. Peel the shrimp and set aside. Cook oysters in their own liquid just until they begin to curl; set aside. Thaw frozen peas. Remove chicken and debone. Strain 2 cups of broth into a skillet, add bell pepper, onions, celery and garlic; cook until tender. Mix together the rice, vegetables and seasonings. Add more broth if needed, to make a very moist mixture. Layer half the rice mixture in a large casserole, sprinkle peas on top, then oysters, shrimp (save a few for top garnish) and chicken. Smooth remaining rice over all. Arrange asparagus spears, pimento (sliced in strips) and shrimp on top. Sprinkle with chopped green onions.
Bake at 350° for 45 minutes - 1 hour.
Serves 10-12.

This makes a beautiful dish!

CHICKEN DEVINE

2 whole chicken breasts
2 pkgs. frozen broccoli spears
8 oz Velveeta cheese, grated
1 can Cream of Mushroom soup
½ tsp. salt
¼ tsp. rosemary
⅛ tsp. pepper
1 tsp. Worcestershire sauce
2 Tbsp. sherry or chicken
  broth
¾-1 cup crumbled potato chips
¾ cup grated cheddar cheese

Boil chicken and cube. Thaw broccoli. Put a layer of broccoli, chicken and cheese, repeat until you use it all. Mix the soup and remaining ingredients except chips and cheddar cheese. Pour over chicken and broccoli. Sprinkle with crumbled chips and grated cheddar cheese. Bake at 350° for 35-40 minutes.
Serves 6-8.

May use a whole chicken if you prefer.

 Words in haste do friendships waste

CHICKEN CASSEROLE

4 lb. chicken
1 (12 oz) pkg. spaghetti
½ stick butter
1 onion, chopped
3-4 cloves garlic, minced
2 small jars mushrooms
1 can Cream of Mushroom soup
1 cup sour cream
¾ cup white wine
¾ cup chicken broth
Salt and pepper to taste

Topping:
1 stack Ritz crackers, crushed
Parmesan cheese
Poppy seed
½ stick melted butter

Boil chicken and debone. Cook spaghetti in broth until done. Save broth. Saute onion, garlic and mushrooms in butter until tender. Add soup, sour cream, wine, ¾ cup broth, salt and pepper to taste.
In a large greased dish, place spaghetti with ½ cup broth, add chicken, then sauce.
Top with cracker crumbs. Sprinkle with Parmesan cheese and poppy seed. Drizzle melted butter over. Bake at 350° for 30-40 minutes. Serves 8.

CHICKEN AND SAUSAGE JAMBALAYA

1 lb. bulk hot sausage
3-3½ lb. chicken
5 cups water
2 Tbsp. flour
1 bell pepper
2 medium onions
2 Tbsp. parsley
1 rib celery
1 tsp. garlic powder
1½ cups rice (uncooked)
¼ tsp. chili powder
¼ tsp. ground cloves
½ tsp. thyme
2 tsp. salt
2 crumbled bay leaves
1½ tsp. Creole seasoning
5 cups chicken stock

Boil chicken in water 1½ hours. Meanwhile, render sausage in a large skillet and remove. Make a dark roux with flour and grease from sausage. Chop the vegetables and add to roux, cook 5 minutes. Add rice, seasonings and sausage. Cook another 5 minutes. Add 5 cups of strained chicken stock and all the chicken. Cook until done (about an hour) over medium low heat, stirring often.
Serves 8.

TURKEY POULET

4 slices toast
8 slices bacon, cooked and
  drained
Leftover turkey
Cream of Mushroom soup
★ Leftover turkey gravy
½ lb. Velveeta cheese

In 4 individual casseroles, layer the toast (if you have leftover dressing, you may use it instead), 2 pieces of bacon and turkey. Heat together the soup, gravy and Velveeta. Spoon sauce over the casseroles. Bake at 375° for 15-20 minutes. Serves 4.

★ If your gravy isn't well seasoned, you'll want to add seasonings.

This is one of Pam's creations. Can you believe such a talented artist has time to create recipes too?!

A good talk with a close friend can solve
problems, or at least put them in perspective,
before they become overpowering.

Seafood

MARY'S CRABMEAT STUFFING

½ cup margarine
1 cup onion, chopped
1 cup celery, chopped
½ cup green pepper, chopped
½ cucumber, chopped
Parsley
½-¾ loaf bread (broken in
  pieces)
1 lb. crabmeat
2 Tbsp. salt
1 tsp. pepper
1 can chicken broth

Melt margarine in skillet, add onion, cook until clear. Add celery, green pepper, then cucumber and parsley. Do not simmer long - leave vegetables slightly crisp. Mix with bread, crabmeat and seasonings. Add chicken broth, mix and stuff in turkey. Place one slice bread in opening to help keep stuffing in turkey. Bake as directed on turkey.

CRAB SOUFFLE

¾ lb. grated cheddar cheese
12 slices white bread
2 cans crabmeat or 1 lb. fresh
  crabmeat
1 can shrimp or ½ lb. boiled
  and cleaned fresh shrimp
8 green onions, chopped
1 tsp. minced garlic
¼ cup chopped bell pepper
2 tsp. chopped parsley
½ cup mayonnaise
4 eggs
3 cups milk
Salt, pepper, cayenne to taste

Cut crust off bread and cube. Mix together the crab, shrimp, onion, garlic, parsley, bell pepper and mayonnaise. Place ½ bread cubes in a buttered casserole dish, add crab-shrimp mixture, then remaining bread cubes. Sprinkle with grated cheese. Beat eggs, add milk, salt, pepper and cayenne. Pour over the layers. Let stand in refrigerator overnight. Bake at 300° for 1½ hours.
Serves 6-8.

Great for brunch or a light dinner.

The supreme happiness in life is the conviction
of being loved for yourself, or, more correctly,
being loved in spite of yourself.

CRABMEAT COOKERY

½ cup chopped onion
½ cup chopped celery
2 tsp. minced garlic
2 Tbsp. chopped parsley
Pinch thyme
1 tsp. salt
½ tsp. pepper
3-4 drops Tabasco
¼ lb. butter
2 cups cornflake crumbs
13 oz evaporated milk
1 lb. crabmeat
1 cup crumbled Ritz crackers
1 Tbsp. flour

Saute onions, celery and garlic in butter. Add thyme, parsley, salt, pepper and Tabasco. Add flour and milk. Heat until hot. Add crabmeat and cornflake crumbs. Pour into a casserole and top with cracker crumbs. Dot with butter. Bake at 375° for 20-25 minutes.

Very Rich!

CRAB QUICHE

1 (10") pie shell
1 egg white, beaten with few
  grains of salt
1 cup shredded Swiss cheese
2 (6½ oz) cans crabmeat,
  drained
3-4 green onions, sliced
4 eggs, well beaten
2 Tbsp. sherry
1¼ cups half and half
½ tsp. salt
½ tsp. pepper
⅛ tsp. cayenne
½ tsp. grated lemon rind
Dash of ground mace
½ cup sliced toasted almonds
Fresh grated nutmeg

Prepare pastry shell in 10" pie plate. Prick lightly and brush with beaten egg white. Sprinkle cheese over shell. Top with the crabmeat and sprinkle with onion. In a medium bowl, combine eggs, sherry, half and half, salt, pepper, cayenne, lemon rind and mace; beat well. Pour over crabmeat and top with almonds. Sprinkle with freshly grated nutmeg. Bake at 325° for 45 minutes or until set. Remove from oven and let stand 10 minutes before serving.

CRABMEAT AU GRATIN

1 large onion, chopped
4 green onions, chopped
3 ribs celery, chopped
2 sticks butter
4 Tbsp. flour
Salt, black pepper, white
  pepper and cayenne to taste
1 large and 1 small can Pet milk
1 Tbsp. Cognac
2 egg yolks
2 lbs. crabmeat
10 oz cheddar cheese, grated

Saute onions and celery in butter. Add flour
and blend - add milk. Remove from heat, add
egg yolks, crabmeat, Cognac and seasonings.
Put in greased au gratin dishes - top with cheese
and bake at 375° for 15 minutes.
(Can also be done in casserole dish - bake 25-
30 minutes.)
Serves 6-8.

STEPHANIE'S CRAWFISH CASSEROLE

2 lbs. crawfish tails
1¼ cups rice, cooked according
  to pkg. directions
1 cup chopped onion
1 cup chopped celery
1 cup chopped green onions
½ cup chopped green pepper
½ cup chopped parsley
1½ sticks butter or margarine
1 can Cream of Mushroom soup
2 cans Cream of Shrimp soup
1 tsp. salt
1 tsp. black pepper
1 tsp. garlic powder
½ tsp. cayenne

Saute vegetables in butter, add crawfish, cook 3
minutes. Add soups, seasonings and rice. Pour
into greased 9x13 casserole. Bake at 350° for
30 minutes.
Serves 8-10.

*Stephanie is another good friend and super
cook as you will discover when you try this
casserole.*

JOE'S GREEK SNAPPER

1½ lbs. snapper fillets
  (or grouper)
¼ cup olive oil
¼ cup butter
1½ cups chopped green onions
½ cup sliced almonds
Salt, pepper, garlic powder
Cayenne

Saute fillets in olive oil and butter. Layer in
baking dish. Pour remainder of oil and butter
over - cover with green onions and almonds.
Sprinkle seasonings over (be generous). Bake
at 350° for 20-30 minutes.

DEE'S CRAWFISH ETOUFEE

3 sticks margarine
1½ cups finely chopped onions
1 cup finely chopped celery
1 cup finely chopped green
  onions
1½ tsp. garlic powder
6 Tbsp. flour
1 (14 oz) can stewed tomatoes
★ 3 cups fish stock or chicken
  broth
3 tsp. salt
1½ tsp. black pepper
¼ tsp. cayenne
10 drops Tabasco
2 Tbsp. Worcestershire sauce
2 lbs. crawfish tails, drained

In a 5 quart pot, saute in margarine the onion, celery, green onion and garlic until vegetables are tender. Add flour, stirring constantly, for 3 minutes. Add tomatoes (mashed a little) plus juice from can. Continue cooking and stirring 5 minutes. Mixture will be golden brown. Blend in stock and seasonings and simmer, stirring occasionally for 10 minutes. Add crawfish and cook slowly for 20 minutes. Adjust seasonings. Serve over rice.
Serves 6-8.

NOTE: This is good made ahead - flavors have a chance to blend.

★ You can use chicken broth but fish stock is better. Recipe follows:

FISH STOCK

2 qts. water
1 large onion, quartered
½ tsp. garlic powder
2 ribs celery
2 lbs. shrimp heads and shells,
  crawfish heads, fish carcasses
  or other seafood shells

Put enough cold water to cover ingredients. Use large pot. Bring to boil, then simmer about 4 hours, adding water as needed to keep at least a quart at all times.
Strain, cool and refrigerate. Freeze in containers if any is left.
I make this anytime I have shrimp and put it in the freezer and then always have it on hand.

BAKED SCAMP

1½ lbs. scamp or flounder
  fillets
3 Tbsp. olive oil
½ cup Italian dressing
Garlic salt
Seasoned pepper
1½ tsp. minced garlic
Parmesan cheese

Place fillets in baking dish and drizzle with olive oil. Pour Italian dressing over and sprinkle with garlic salt and seasoned pepper★. Bake at 350° for about 15 minutes or until nearly done. Remove from oven, cover with Parmesan cheese and bake an additional 5-10 minutes or until fish flakes easily.
Serves 4.

★ Be very generous with the seasonings.

Thanks again, Dad!

LEMON-BROILED FISH FILLETS

1½-2 lbs. trout fillets or bass
  fillets
1-1½ sticks butter, melted
4 Tbsp. lemon juice
Salt, pepper, garlic powder
McCormicks lemon-pepper

Place fillets in broiler-pan. Season with salt, pepper, garlic and lemon-pepper. Mix butter and lemon juice. Pour, slowly, over fillets. Let set for 30 minutes-1 hour. Broil 8-10 minutes each side or until fish flakes easily.
Serves 4-6.

This is very lemony and one of my most recent creations. It is now one of Sam's favorites.

OYSTERS ALBERTA

1 qt. oysters
1 stick butter
½ cup green onions, chopped
2 Tbsp. parsley, chopped
½ cup grated cheddar cheese
½ cup Italian bread crumbs
Tabasco, garlic salt, pepper
  to taste
Additional bread crumbs for
  topping

Cook onion and parsley in butter, add seasonings. Add cheese and oysters and cook over medium heat until oysters begin to curl. Add bread crumbs and place in a casserole. Top with more bread crumbs. Bake at 350° for 15 minutes.
Serves 4.

BAKED OYSTERS

Fresh oysters
Saltine cracker crumbs
Garlic salt
Seasoned pepper
Butter
Parmesan cheese

Put oysters in a baking dish or ramekin. Sprinkle with cracker crumbs. Dot with butter. Sprinkle with garlic salt and seasoned pepper. Bake at 350° until the edges begin to curl. Remove from oven and sprinkle with Parmesan cheese. Return to oven for about 5 more minutes.

My dad created this one; it keeps our mouths watering when we start heading for Florida.

It is better to have loved and lost
than never to have loved at all.

BAKED SHRIMP

2 lbs. shrimp, cleaned and butterflied
1 pkg. Escort crackers, crushed
2 tsp. sherry
1 stick melted butter
Paprika
Garlic salt
Seasoned pepper
Cayenne

Pat shrimp dry and arrange in greased baking dish. Mix cracker crumbs with sherry and sprinkle over shrimp. Drizzle melted butter over top. Sprinkle with seasonings (to taste). Bake at 400° for 15-20 minutes.
Serves 3-4.

DAD'S SKILLET CREOLE

¼ lb. bacon, chopped
2 Tbsp. minced garlic
3 ribs celery, chopped
1 onion, chopped
2 bell peppers, chopped
3 fresh tomatoes, chopped
1 tsp. Italian seasoning
1 tsp. gumbo file
½ tsp. Creole Seasoning
Garlic salt, pepper to taste
1 can Rotel tomatoes with chiles, chopped
2 lbs. shrimp, fantailed

In large skillet, saute bacon with garlic, celery, onion, bell pepper and tomatoes - add Italian seasoning, file, Creole Seasoning, garlic salt and pepper. Add chopped Rotel tomatoes and shrimp. Cook until shrimp are pink - vegetables should not be too soft. Serve over rice.
Serves 4-6.

Variations: add Italian sausage or crabmeat or both. Good!

My dad just decided to throw this together one day. Try this and you'll thank him as much as I do!

DEE'S BAR-B-QUE SHRIMP

8 dozen large shrimp
Salt, pepper, garlic

Sauce:
2 sticks butter
½ cup lemon juice
2 tsp. Worcestershire sauce
1 tsp. oregano
½ tsp. tarragon
1 bay leaf
1 tsp. basil
4 green onions, finely chopped

Peel and place shrimp on foil-lined pan (about 2" deep). Season with salt, pepper and garlic. Combine all sauce ingredients. Pour over shrimp and marinate 30 minutes or more. Broil - basting with sauce - until done.
Serves 6-8.

Sauce is good for dipping with French bread.

ELEGANT SHRIMP SANDWICHES

½ cup chopped green onions
2 tsp. minced garlic
½ cup butter
½ cup margarine
2½ lbs. large shrimp, peeled
  and deveined
1 tsp. lemon juice
1 Tbsp. white wine
½ tsp. salt
¼ tsp. seasoned pepper
½ tsp. dried dill weed
1 Tbsp. chopped parsley
3 drops Tabasco
Cayenne
3 French rolls, split and toasted

Saute onions and garlic in butter and margarine. Add shrimp, lemon juice, wine, salt and pepper. Cook over medium heat about 5 minutes, stirring often. Stir in dill weed, parsley, Tabasco and cayenne. Spoon shrimp mixture over the toasted rolls and serve immediately. Serves 6.

SPICY SHRIMP CASSEROLE

4 lbs. shrimp, peeled
1 can Golden Mushroom soup
1 can Rotel tomatoes
1 box Mahatma Golden Rice
  (use both pkgs.)
½ stick oleo or butter
1 large onion, chopped
1 bell pepper, chopped
1 medium can mushrooms
Salt, pepper to taste

Cook rice as directed on package. Saute chopped onion and bell pepper in oleo. Add shrimp and cook until shrimp are pink. Add soup and Rotel tomatoes. Simmer 15 minutes. Mix cooked rice, mushrooms and shrimp. Taste, adjust seasonings. Put in greased oblong dish - bake at 350° for 30-40 minutes. Serves 8.

This recipe comes from a dear friend and wonderful cook, Roberta.

Happiness is a hard thing because it is only achieved by making others happy.

SHRIMP CREOLE

½ cup vegetable oil
½ cup flour
1 large onion, finely chopped
3 (8 oz) cans tomato sauce
3 cans water
Salt, pepper, garlic powder and
  basil to taste
2 bay leaves
2-3 Tbsp. Worcestershire sauce
¼ cup ketchup
1 bell pepper, cut in 6 pieces
1 bunch chopped green onions
½ bunch chopped parsley
⅛ tsp. cayenne
3 lbs. shrimp, peeled (small to
  medium size)

In a 4 quart black iron pot, add oil and flour. Cook on medium heat, stirring constantly until light golden brown. Turn heat to low and add onion. Cover and cook until onion is soft (approx. 5 minutes). Return heat to medium - add all ingredients except shrimp. When sauce starts to bubble, turn heat to low, cover and cook, stirring occasionally, 30-45 minutes. Add shrimp and cook for about 30 minutes. Taste and adjust seasonings. Serve over rice. Serves 6-8.

This is good made early in the day so it can set a few hours. Spices blend better.

Different but very good!

TERESA'S BROILED SHRIMP

24 large shrimp
4 Tbsp. Worcestershire sauce
4 Tbsp. lemon juice
Garlic salt with parsley
Seasoned pepper
8 slices bacon

Butter Sauce:
1 stick melted butter
4 Tbsp. lemon juice
Garlic salt
Seasoned pepper

Clean, devein and butterfly shrimp, leaving tails intact. Sprinkle with garlic salt, pepper, Worcestershire and lemon. Marinate for 1 hour in refrigerator.

Cut bacon in 3 pieces and wrap around each shrimp. Use a toothpick to keep together. Place shrimp in a baking dish.

Combine butter, lemon juice, garlic salt and pepper. Pour over shrimp. Broil 5 minutes on one side - turn and broil 5 minutes on other side or until shrimp are pink and bacon is crisp. Serves 4.

Great with rice pilaf and green salad.

STUFFED SHRIMP

24 jumbo shrimp
1 cup crumbled Escort
  crackers
3 cups cornbread stuffing
3 Tbsp. butter
1 Tbsp. lemon juice
½ cup minced onion
½ cup minced green pepper
⅓ cup minced celery
1 egg, beaten
1 tsp. minced garlic
Salt, pepper, cayenne to taste
2 drops Tabasco
3 cups chicken broth

Mix together:
1 Tbsp. paprika
1 cup cornmeal

Saute onion, pepper, celery and garlic in butter. Add stuffing and all ingredients except shrimp, paprika and cornmeal. Mix well. Cook over medium heat until moist and firm. Mix paprika and cornmeal and set aside. Peel, devein and split shrimp, leaving tail intact. Form ball around shrimp with the stuffing mixture. Roll in cornmeal mixture and fry until golden brown. Serves 4.

OPEN FACE TUNAWICHES

6½ oz can chunk white tuna
4 green onions, chopped
½ cup grated cheddar cheese
3-4 Tbsp. mayonnaise
Salt, pepper
4 hamburger buns

Combine tuna, onions, cheese, mayonnaise, salt and pepper. Spread on bottom of hamburger buns. Broil until cheese melts, also toast top of bun.
Serves 4.

A little different taste!

The light of friendship is like the light of phosphorus, seen when all around is dark.

Cakes
And
Pies

STRAWBERRY - PECAN CAKE

1 white cake mix
1 small pkg. strawberry jello
3 Tbsp. flour
½ cup water
1 cup light oil
4 eggs
1 small box frozen strawberries
1 cup coconut
1 cup finely chopped pecans
1 box powdered sugar
1 stick butter
½ cup frozen strawberries,
  thawed and drained
½ cup finely chopped pecans
½ cup coconut

Combine cake mix, jello, flour; add water and oil. Blend well. Add eggs, one at a time; beat well after each. Add strawberries, 1 cup coconut and 1 cup pecans. Pour into 3 greased and floured 9" cake pans. Bake at 350° for 25-30 minutes. Cool.

Cream the powdered sugar and butter. Blend in ½ cup berries, pecans and coconut. Ice cake and keep refrigerated.

BLACK FOREST TORTE

40 Ritz crackers, crushed fine
2 tsp. baking powder
2 cups finely chopped pecans
2 cups sugar
6 stiffly beaten egg whites
2 tsp. vanilla
½ pt. whipping cream, whipped
Chocolate bar, grated

Mix together cracker crumbs, baking powder, pecans and sugar. Fold into egg whites with vanilla. Grease 3 cake pans and line with foil. Evenly distribute mixture between the 3 pans. Bake at 350° until crisp, 10-15 minutes. Immediately remove from pan or it will stick. Put together with whipped cream and cover top with whipped cream and grated chocolate. Freezes well.

PINA COLADA CAKE

1 yellow cake mix
1 small can Coco Lopez coconut syrup
1 can condensed milk
1 large can crushed pineapple,
  drained
1 (8 oz) Cool Whip

Make a 9x13 cake according to directions. Mix together coconut syrup and condensed milk. Punch holes in the cake with a fork. Pour milk mixture over the cake. Spread drained pineapple over the top. Ice with Cool Whip (may top with coconut if desired). Refrigerate.

WATERGATE CAKE

Cake:
1 pkg. white cake mix
¾ cup Crisco oil
3 eggs
1 cup 7-Up or club soda
1 pkg. pistachio instant
 pudding
1 cup chopped nuts
½ cup coconut

Cover Up Icing:
2 envelopes (3 oz each) Dream
 Whip, dry
1 pkg. pistachio instant
 pudding
¾ cup chopped nuts
½ cup coconut
1½ cups milk

Cake:
Combine in order given. Mix well. Pour into a greased and floured 9x13 pan. Bake at 350° for 35-40 minutes.
Icing:
Combine Dream Whip (dry) and pudding mix. Add milk. Beat with mixer until thick. Spread on cake and sprinkle coconut and nuts on top. Keep refrigerated.

CHOCOLATE ECLAIR CAKE

2 small pkgs. French Vanilla
 instant pudding
3 cups milk
1 (8 oz) carton Cool Whip
Graham crackers (all but one
 pkg. out of box)

Topping:
2 squares Bakers semi-sweet
 chocolate
6 Tbsp. margarine
2 Tbsp. white Karo
1 tsp. vanilla
1½ cups powdered sugar
3 Tbsp. milk

Mix milk and pudding well, fold in Cool Whip. Line oblong pan (9x12) in single layers with crackers. Spread ½ the pudding over the crackers, repeating until all is used, ending with a layer of crackers.
Topping:
Melt chocolate with margarine and syrup. Bring to boil. Remove from heat. Add vanilla, sugar and milk. Mix and pour over eclair mixture. Refrigerate at least 10 hours before serving - 24 hours even better.

Stand back and wait for raves!

 Be what you wish others to become.

MANDARIN ORANGE CAKE

1 box butter flavor cake mix
1 can mandarin oranges
4 eggs
½ cup oil
1 (20 oz) can crushed pineapple (undrained)
1 small box vanilla instant
  pudding
1 (12 oz) carton Cool Whip

Beat together the cake mix, oranges (do not drain), eggs and oil. Pour into a greased 9x13 pan or 2 (9") cake pans. Bake at 350° for 25 minutes. Cool. Remove from pans.
Combine pineapple with the pudding mix and fold into Cool Whip. Ice cake and refrigerate overnight.

A luscious summer cake!

RED VELVET CAKE

1½ cups sugar
½ cup shortening
2 eggs
2 cups flour
1 tsp. salt
2 Tbsp. cocoa
1 cup buttermilk
2 oz red food coloring
1½ tsp. vanilla
1 tsp. soda in 1 Tbsp. vinegar

Icing:
1 cup milk
1 cup sugar
¼ tsp. salt
¼ cup flour
1 cup butter
2 tsp. vanilla
1 cup flaked coconut

Cream sugar and shortening; add eggs and beat well. Sift flour, salt and cocoa 3 times and add alternately to creamed mixture with buttermilk. Add vanilla and coloring. Fold in soda and vinegar, but do not beat. Bake in 3 (9") greased and well-floured pans at 350° for 25-30 minutes.
Icing:
Mix flour and salt with milk until blended; cook slowly until very thick. Cool thoroughly! Cream butter and sugar until fluffy; then add to cooled mixture and beat well (looks like whipped cream). Add vanilla. Put on cake and garnish with coconut (be sure that your cake is cold so the butter icing won't melt).

This is a nice cake to make on Valentine's Day. Bake in 3 (9") heart-shaped pans. My family loves it.

GWEN'S HUCKLEBERRY CAKE

1 Angel Food cake mix
1 tsp. vanilla flavoring
1 tsp. almond flavoring
½ pt. whipping cream
2 Tbsp. powdered sugar
½ cup huckleberry jam (or blueberry)
½ small pkg. coconut

Prepare cake mix according to directions, adding vanilla and almond flavoring.
Line a cookie sheet with wax paper. Pour mixture in and bake at 350° for 15 minutes or until lightly browned.
Sprinkle a dish towel with powdered sugar. Flip cake out on dish towel. Peel off wax paper and roll up. Cool in refrigerator.
Whip cream very stiff with 2 tablespoons powdered sugar. Unroll cooled cake. Spread with jam, then with ⅓ of the whipped cream. Sprinkle with coconut - roll up. Ice with remaining whipped cream and sprinkle coconut on top.

Gwen introduced me to the huckleberry bush. I picked plenty to have jam on hand for this cake. It's as pretty as it is good!

CHOCOLATE MARBLE CHEESECAKE

½ cup chocolate wafer crumbs
1 Tbsp. soft butter
3 (8 oz) pkgs. cream cheese
1 cup sugar
1½ tsp. vanilla
5 eggs
2 oz semi-sweet chocolate, melted

Chocolate-sour cream frosting:
1 (6 oz) pkg. semi-sweet chocolate chips
½ cup sour cream
Dash salt

Combine crumbs and butter - press in the bottom of a lightly greased 10" Springform pan.
Combine cream cheese, sugar and vanilla - beat until smooth. Add eggs, one at a time. Set 1 cup of this mixture aside. Pour the rest into pan. Fold melted chocolate into reserved 1 cup mixture and spoon onto batter. Swirl with a knife. Bake at 300° for 50-55 minutes. Cool. Refrigerate 2 hours. Frost top and sides. Chill at least 4 hours.
Frosting:
Melt chocolate in double-boiler, add sour cream and salt. Beat with a wooden spoon.

PRUNE SPICE CAKE

3 eggs
1½ cups sugar
1 cup Crisco oil
1 cup buttermilk
2¼ cups flour
½ tsp. salt.
1 tsp. baking powder
1 tsp. soda
1 tsp. nutmeg
1 tsp. cinnamon
1 heaping cup cooked prunes, chopped
1 cup nuts, chopped

Icing:
1 box powdered sugar
½ stick melted butter
1 (8 oz) pkg. cream cheese
1 tsp. vanilla

Beat eggs, add sugar and beat well - add oil - beat in buttermilk. Sift flour, spices, salt, soda and baking powder and add gradually to first mixture. Add prunes and chopped nuts. Bake in a well greased and floured 9x13 pan for 35 minutes at 350°. Let cool - then ice.
Icing:
Mix ingredients together in bowl. Beat with mixer until fluffy.

Don't let the prunes keep you from trying this cake. It's delicious - you'd never know the cake had prunes in it - moist!

APPLESAUCE CAKE

2¼ cups flour
1 (15 oz) jar applesauce
1¼ cups sugar
⅔ cup shortening
⅓ cup milk
2 eggs
2 tsp. baking soda
1 tsp. cinnamon
½ tsp. salt
½ tsp. nutmeg
½ tsp. ground cloves
1 cup white raisins
½ cup chopped pecans

In a large bowl, measure all ingredients except raisins and nuts. Beat with a mixer on low speed until well mixed, scraping bowl with a spatula. Beat on high 3 minutes. Stir in raisins and nuts. Pour batter into a greased and floured 9x13 or bundt pan. Bake at 350° for 40-45 minutes or until a toothpick inserted in center comes out clean. Cool pan on wire rack.

Great to pack in lunches!

APPLE CAKE

1½ cups oil
2 cups sugar
3 eggs, beaten
3 tsp. vanilla extract
1 tsp. black walnut extract
3 cups flour
1½ tsp. baking soda
1 tsp. salt
1 tsp. ground nutmeg
1½ cups chopped pecans
3 large, Delicious apples, diced
  fine

Combine oil, sugar, eggs, vanilla and black walnut extracts in a large bowl. Stir by hand until smooth. Add flour, soda, salt and nutmeg, beat by hand. Add nuts and apples. Grease and flour a bundt pan, pour in mixture. Bake at 325° for 1½-2 hours. Cool 30 minutes.
Will keep up to 3 weeks. Good served with whipped cream, sprinkled with nutmeg.

LEMON CAKE

1 lemon cake mix
1 small pkg. lemon jello
½ cup oil
½ cup water
4 eggs

Lemon filling:
4½ Tbsp. cornstarch
1 cup sugar
1¼ cups cold water
2 egg yolks, slightly beaten
1 tsp. salt
2 tsp. grated lemon rind
¼ cup lemon juice
1 Tbsp. butter

Cake:
Blend cake mix, jello, oil, water and eggs until smooth with mixer. Beat for 5 minutes. Pour into 2 greased and floured cake pans. Bake at 325° for 45-60 minutes.
Lemon filling:
Stir cornstarch and sugar in pan until clear. Gradually add water, stirring until smooth. After each addition of water, cook on low heat, stirring constantly, until thick and clear.
Vigorously stir a small amount of hot mixture into egg yolks, then add egg mixture and salt to pan and cook a few minutes more over low heat.
Remove from heat and add grated lemon rind, juice and butter. Spread between layers and on top of cake.

CREOLE CAKE

1 cup margarine
2 cups sugar
6 eggs
12 oz vanilla wafers,
  crumbled in blender
½ cup milk
1 cup chopped nuts
7 oz Angel Flake coconut

Cream margarine, sugar and eggs. Add milk and vanilla wafer crumbs, alternately. Fold in nuts and coconut. Bake in a well-greased bundt or tube cake pan at 300° for at least 1½ hours (may take a little longer).

A very moist cake. Keeps well and improves with age. Also good with whipped cream or sweetened sour cream. Delicious!

WHISKEY CAKE

1 pkg. yellow cake mix
1 large pkg. instant vanilla
  pudding
½ cup Crisco oil
½ cup water
½ cup whiskey
4 eggs
¾ cup chopped pecans

Sauce:
1 stick butter
1 cup sugar
¼ cup water
¼ cup whiskey

Mix cake mix, pudding, oil, water, ½ cup whiskey and eggs. Beat 10 minutes. Grease bundt pan, pour pecans on bottom of pan. Pour batter over pecans. Bake 1 hour at 325°. When done, let cool a few minutes, then poke holes in cake with icepick. Pour sauce on cake and COOL COMPLETELY before removing from pan.
Sauce:
Boil butter, sugar and water until all sugar has melted, add whiskey. Pour slowly over cake so holes can absorb sauce. Use all of the sauce. Keeps well.

Delicious! Don't expect it to last long, though! Men love it!

GOLDEN CAKE

1 pkg. yellow cake mix
½ cup oil
4 eggs
1 cup canned pumpkin
¾ cup sugar
1 tsp. cinnamon
Dash nutmeg
¼ cup water

Put cake mix in large bowl. Make an indention in center and pour in oil and 1 egg. Mix, then add rest of eggs, one at a time, beating after each one. Add pumpkin, sugar and spices, then water. Bake in greased and floured tube pan at 350° for 50-60 minutes. Cool before removing from pan. Very moist!

This comes from my sweet neighbor, Barbara. She says cooking isn't her "strong suit". This cake proves different! Try it - you'll agree - it's terrific!

SOUR CREAM POUND CAKE

½ lb. butter
3 cups sugar
3 cups flour
½ pt. sour cream
6 eggs
¼ tsp. soda
½ tsp. lemon flavoring
½ tsp. almond flavoring
1 tsp. vanilla flavoring

Let butter and eggs reach room temperature. Sift flour; then sift again with soda. Cream butter and sugar. Add eggs, one at a time (beat at same speed as creaming butter and sugar). Add flour, alternating with sour cream. Lower mixer speed and add flavorings. Pour into greased and floured bundt pan. Bake at 325° for 1 hour and 15 minutes.

APRICOT BRANDY POUND CAKE

1 cup margarine (2 sticks)
3 cups sugar
6 eggs
3 cups flour
½ tsp. salt
¼ tsp. soda
1 cup sour cream
½ tsp. lemon flavoring
¼ tsp. almond flavoring
1 tsp. orange flavoring
½ tsp. rum flavoring
1 tsp. vanilla flavoring
1 cup apricot brandy

Icing:
4 cups powdered sugar
6 Tbsp. melted margarine
1 tsp. vanilla
¼ cup apricot brandy

Cream margarine until light. Add sugar, a cup at a time. Cream until light and fluffy. Add eggs, one at a time, beating after each one. Beat 3 minutes after last egg is added. Sift flour and measure. Sift again with salt and soda. Combine the sour cream and flavorings. Add flour mixture and flavored sour cream alternately to the batter. Blend well. Fold in apricot brandy. Bake in well-greased tube or bundt pan at 350° for 70 minutes or until done.

Good without icing; but if icing is preferred, combine sugar, margarine, vanilla and brandy and ice cake. Keeps in refrigerator for weeks.

Very good cake!

COCONUT POUND CAKE

2 sticks oleo or butter
½ cup Crisco
3 cups sugar
6 eggs
½ tsp. almond flavoring
1 tsp. coconut flavoring
3 cups flour
1 cup milk
1 can coconut
1 tsp. salt

Glaze:
1 cup sugar
½ cup water
2 tsp. coconut flavoring

Cream oleo, Crisco and sugar until fluffy. Add eggs, one at a time, beating after each one. Add flavoring. Mix well. Add flour (to which salt has been added) and milk alternately. Stir in coconut. Put in a greased tube pan. Bake for 1 hour and 15 minutes at 325° or until done. Makes a big cake. Glaze, if desired.
Glaze:
Mix sugar, water and flavoring. Boil 1 minute. Pour over cake.

CHOCOLATE ZUCCHINI CAKE

2½ cups flour
½ cup cocoa
2½ tsp. baking powder
1 tsp. salt
1½ tsp. soda
1½ tsp. cinnamon
¾ cup margarine
2 cups sugar
3 eggs
2 cups (½ lb.) grated unpeeled zucchini
2 tsp. grated orange peel
2 tsp. vanilla
½ cup milk
1 cup ground pecans

Glaze:
¾ cup powdered sugar
1 Tbsp. orange juice
½ tsp. grated orange peel

Mix first 6 ingredients together. Set aside. Cream margarine and sugar, add eggs. Stir in zucchini, orange peel and vanilla. Stir in flour mixture and milk, alternately. Add pecans. Pour into greased 12-cup bundt pan. Bake 1 hour. Cool 15 minutes. Invert to remove from pan. Spread with glaze.

Very different - very good!

7-UP POUND CAKE

2 sticks oleo
½ cup Crisco
3 cups sugar
5 eggs
3 cups flour (sifted twice)
1 (6 oz) regular bottle 7-Up
1 tsp. vanilla
1 tsp. lemon extract
½ tsp. almond extract

Cream together the oleo, Crisco and sugar. Add eggs, one at a time, and beat well after each one. Alternate flour and 7-Up, beating well after each addition. Add flavorings. Pour into greased tube or bundt pan. Bake at 350° for 45 minutes. Reduce heat to 300° for 35 minutes or until done.

This is one of my favorite pound cakes. The recipe came from my grandmother.

BOTY'S CHOCOLATE SHEET CAKE

2 cups sugar
2 cups flour
¼ tsp. salt
2 sticks margarine
4 Tbsp. cocoa
1 cup water
2 eggs, well beaten
½ cup buttermilk
1 tsp. soda
1 tsp. baking powder
1 Tbsp. vanilla

Icing:
1 stick margarine
4 Tbsp. cocoa
6 Tbsp. Pet milk
1 tsp. vanilla
Pinch salt
1 box powdered sugar
1 cup chopped toasted pecans

Put sugar, flour and salt in a bowl.
In saucepan, put margarine, cocoa and water. Bring to a boil and pour over first mixture. Add eggs, buttermilk, soda, baking powder and vanilla. Mix well. Bake in greased 9x13 pan at 400° for 25 minutes or until done. Make icing and spread over cake after removing from oven and while still warm.
Icing:
In saucepan, combine margarine, cocoa, Pet milk, vanilla and salt. Bring to a boil and then add powdered sugar and pecans.

ONE PAN CHOCOLATE CAKE

3 cups flour
2 cups sugar
2 tsp. soda
6 Tbsp. cocoa
½ tsp. salt
2 Tbsp. vinegar
1 Tbsp. vanilla
2 cups cold water
¾ cup salad oil

Chocolate Glaze:
2 squares unsweetened
  chocolate
1 tsp. butter
1 cup sifted powdered sugar
3 Tbsp. water
½ tsp. vanilla

Sift all dry ingredients into an ungreased 9x13 pan. Make 3 holes in mixture. Pour oil in one hole, vinegar in one and vanilla into the third. Cover with the water and stir well with a fork. Make sure the dry ingredients are mixed thoroughly. Bake at 350° for 25 minutes. Glaze right away - while cake is still hot.
Glaze:
Melt chocolate with butter over low heat. Stir in powdered sugar; beat in water until smooth. Add vanilla. Pour over cake.

This cake gets more moist each day. Doesn't last long, though. A family favorite.

LIGHT FRUITCAKE

1 lb. butter
2¼ cups sugar
6 eggs
4 cups flour (reserve ½ cup to
  dredge fruit in)
1 tsp. baking powder
4 tsp. lemon flavoring
1 Tbsp. butter flavoring
★8-12 oz green and red
  candied cherries
★8-12 oz green and red
  candied pineapple
½ lb. white raisins
5 cups chopped pecans
2 Tbsp. whiskey

Cream together butter, sugar and eggs. Add flour, baking powder and flavorings. Dredge fruit in ½ cup reserved flour, stir into mixture. Add pecans and whiskey, stir well. Bake at 250°. It takes 3½-4 hours for a bundt pan or 1½ hours for the small loaf pans. Will make 8 small loaves.
★Use more or less fruit according to your preference.

Gwen got me hooked on this one!

ICE BOX FRUITCAKE

1 (12 oz) box vanilla wafers, crushed
½ lb. candied red cherries, halved
½ lb. candied green pineapple, diced
1 lb. pecan halves
2 large eggs
½ cup sugar
1 small can evaporated milk
¼ tsp. salt

Put crushed vanilla wafers in a large bowl. Add cherry halves, diced pineapple and pecans; mix well. Beat eggs in another bowl, add sugar, milk and salt. Mix well. Add to first mixture, blending well. Pour into a greased tube pan and press firmly. Bake at 325° for 1 hour. Cool, then refrigerate.

ARONOWITZ FRUITCAKE

1 lb. pitted dates
1 lb. chopped pecans
½ lb. candied cherries, cut up
½ lb. candied pineapple, cut up
1 cup sugar
1 cup flour
2 tsp. baking powder
½ tsp. salt
1 tsp. nutmeg
4 eggs
1 tsp. vanilla

Line angel food pan with heavy brown paper. Cut up candied fruit and mix with chopped pecans. Sift dry ingredients together and mix with the fruit and nuts. Beat eggs with vanilla and pour over other ingredients. Pack into pan. Bake 2 hours at 250°. Cool cake before removing from pan. Let mellow a week, if possible.

CHOCOLATE CHESS PIE

1 stick margarine
2 squares bitter chocolate
4 eggs
2 cups sugar
1 Tbsp. flour
1 tsp. vanilla
1 unbaked 9" pie shell

Melt margarine and chocolate. Beat eggs; add sugar, flour and vanilla. Stir in chocolate mixture. Pour into pie shell and bake at 450° for 10 minutes, reduce heat to 350° and bake 30 minutes.

Tip: To keep pie crust crisp, bake at 400° for 5 minutes before you put filling in. You must prick the pie crust with a fork before baking.

HERSHEY BAR PIE

6 Hershey bars (with or without almonds)
½ cup milk
16 marshmallows
½ pt. whipping cream
1 (8") pie shell, baked and cooled

Melt Hersheys, milk and marshmallows together in top of double boiler. Let cool completely. Beat whipping cream until peaks form. Fold into cooled chocolate mixture and pour into pie shell. Keep refrigerated until ready to serve.

Yummy!

MARY ANN'S CHOCOLATE PIE

1½ cups sugar
½ cup cocoa
6 Tbsp. flour
½ tsp. salt
3 cups milk
3 eggs, separated
1 Tbsp. butter
1½ tsp. vanilla
¼ tsp. cream of tartar
6 Tbsp. sugar
1 (10") baked pie shell

In saucepan, mix together 1½ cups sugar, cocoa, flour and salt. Gradually stir in milk. Cook over medium heat, stirring constantly, until mixture thickens and boils. Boil one minute. Remove from heat. Gradually stir at least half of hot mixture into the 3 egg yolks, slightly beaten. Blend into hot mixture in saucepan. Boil one more minute, stirring constantly. Remove from heat and blend in butter and vanilla. Pour into baked pie shell.
Blend egg whites with cream of tartar at high speed. Beat until frothy. Gradually beat in 6 tablespoons sugar and beat until stiff and glossy. Cover pie with meringue and bake at 375° until browned.

BANANA CARAMEL PIE

1 can condensed milk
Graham cracker crust
2 medium bananas
9½ oz Cool Whip
¼-½ cup toasted chopped
  pecans or almonds
1 Heath bar, grated

Place the can of unopened condensed milk in a saucepan and cover with boiling water. Boil for 3 hours, keeping the can covered with water. Cool. Spread sliced bananas over crust and cover with caramelized milk. Top with Cool Whip. Sprinkle with nuts and grated Heath bar. Refrigerate at least 4 hours.

BANANA SPLIT PIE

2 cups graham cracker crumbs
1 stick melted margarine
2 sticks margarine
2 cups powdered sugar
3 eggs
5 sliced bananas
2 cups sliced strawberries
1 can crushed pineapple,
  drained
½ cup chopped toasted pecans
9½ oz Cool Whip

Mix cracker crumbs and melted margarine together. Pat into a 9x13 pan.
Beat 2 sticks margarine, sugar and eggs 20 minutes (DO NOT UNDERBEAT). Spread over crust. Cover with bananas, strawberries and pineapple. Spread Cool Whip over fruit. Sprinkle pecans on top. Refrigerate overnight.

KEY LIME PIE

1 envelope unflavored gelatin
1 cup sugar
¼ tsp. salt
4 eggs, separated
½ cup lime juice
¼ cup water
1 tsp. grated lime peel
Green food coloring
1 cup whipping cream, whipped
1 baked 9" pie shell
2 Tbsp. grated pistachio nuts
1 cup whipping cream, whipped

Mix gelatin, ½ cup sugar and salt in pan. Beat together egg yolks, lime juice and water. Stir into gelatin mixture. Cook and stir over medium heat just until mixture comes to a boil. Remove from heat, stir in grated peel and a few drops of food coloring. Chill, stirring once, until mixture mounds. Beat egg whites until soft peaks form. Gradually add ½ cup sugar, beating to stiff peaks. Fold gelatin mixture into egg whites. Fold in 1 cup whipped cream. Pour into pie shell, chill until firm.
Spread with remaining 1 cup whipping cream and edge with additional grated lime peel and grated pistachio nuts. Chill.

This is such a good pie. Thanks to Monya for sharing her brother, Steve's, talents with us.

DELICIOUS CHERRY PIE

Filling:
3 (16 oz) pkgs. frozen dark
  sweet cherries
1¼ cups sugar, divided
½ cup cornstarch
3 Tbsp. water
3 Tbsp. butter
1½ tsp. almond flavoring

Pie Crust:
2 cups all-purpose flour
½ tsp. salt
½ tsp. cinnamon
⅔ cup shortening
½ cup cold milk

Filling:
Combine 1 cup sugar and cornstarch in a saucepan; stir to remove lumps - add water. Cook over medium heat until smooth, stirring constantly. Add remaining sugar, cherries, (partially thawed), butter and almond flavoring; stir until butter melts. Pour into pie shell. Top with crust. Bake at 375° for 50-55 minutes.

Crust:
Combine flour, salt and cinnamon in bowl; cut in shortening with pastry blender or fork until mixture resembles cornmeal. Sprinkle milk evenly over mixture. Stir with a fork until all dry ingredients are moistened. Shape dough in a ball. Refrigerate 30 minutes.

Divide in half and roll each to fit a 10" pie plate.

The cinnamon adds a nice touch with any fruit pie.

STRAWBERRY MERINGUE

3 egg whites
⅔ cup sugar
8-10 crushed saltines
½ tsp. baking powder
½ cup ground pecans
1 pt. strawberries, sliced
1 cup whipping cream
1 Tbsp. powdered sugar
½ tsp. almond extract
Whole berries for garnish

Beat egg whites until frothy; gradually add sugar and beat until stiff peaks form. Fold in crushed saltines, baking powder and pecans. Pour into a greased 9" pie plate. being sure to coat sides. Bake at 300° for 25-30 minutes. Cool.

Place sliced berries into cooled shell. Whip cream with powdered sugar and almond extract, spoon over strawberries. Garnish with whole berries. Chill.

GINNY'S PINEAPPLE PIE

½ cup butter
1½ cups sugar
1½ Tbsp. flour
3 eggs
½ tsp. vanilla
1 cup crushed pineapple,
  drained
1 (9") unbaked pie shell

Cream butter and sugar, add flour. Beat eggs and slowly add to mixture. Add vanilla and pineapple. Pour into unbaked pie shell. Bake at 350° for one hour.

STRAWBERRY PIE

1 pt. fresh strawberries
1 cup sugar
1¼ cups water
3 Tbsp. cornstarch
1 small pkg. strawberry jello
9" pie shell, baked

Wash and drain whole strawberries. Cook together, over medium heat, the sugar, water and cornstarch, stirring constantly, until thickened. Remove from heat and add jello.
Place strawberries in cooled pie shell and pour jello mixture over. Chill until set.
Serve with whipped cream or Cool Whip.

TEXAS PIE

3 eggs
1¾ cups sugar
¾ stick margarine
2 Tbsp. flour
2 Tbsp. lemon juice
1 small can crushed pineapple,
  undrained
1 cup coconut
1 tsp. vanilla
1 (9") unbaked pie shell

Beat eggs, sugar and flour. Add lemon juice, coconut, softened margarine, pineapple and vanilla. Pour into unbaked pie shell. Bake at 425° for 15 minutes, reduce heat to 350° and bake for 45 minutes.

ICE CREAM PIE

24 Oreo cookies, crushed in blender
⅓ cup melted butter
½ gallon chocolate ice cream
3 oz unsweetened chocolate
1 cup sugar
Dash salt
2 Tbsp. butter
1½ cups evaporated milk
½ tsp. vanilla
8 oz carton Cool Whip
½ oz Kahlua
½-1 cup toasted pecans or almonds

Combine cookie crumbs with melted butter. Press into a 9x13 pan. Spread with softened ice cream, cover and freeze.
Melt chocolate and 2 tablespoons butter over low heat. Add sugar, salt and milk. Cook and stir until thickened. Remove from heat and add vanilla. Chill until completely cool. Spread on top of ice cream layer and return to freezer.
Combine thawed Cool Whip with Kahlua. Spread over frozen chocolate layer, sprinkle with nuts and freeze. Remove from freezer a few minutes before serving.

STRAWBERRY ICE CREAM PIE

Filling:
1 regular size pkg. strawberry jello
1¼ cups boiling water
1 pt. vanilla ice cream
1 cup drained strawberries (frozen berries will do)

Pie Crust:
1½ cups graham cracker crumbs
¼ cup powdered sugar
1 tsp. cinnamon
6 Tbsp. oleo, melted

Filling:
Mix jello and water. Stir in ice cream until melted. Chill until very thick and then fold in berries. Pour into crust. Chill until serving time.
Crust:
Mix crumbs, sugar, cinnamon and oleo - press into 9" pie plate.

Very easy - very good!

BUTTERMILK PIE

1 stick margarine
2 cups sugar
3 Tbsp. flour
3 eggs
1 cup buttermilk
½ tsp. lemon extract or 1 tsp. vanilla and grated nutmeg
1 unbaked pie shell

Mix flour and sugar; cream with margarine. Add eggs, one at a time, beating thoroughly after each. Add the buttermilk and lemon extract (or vanilla and nutmeg). Pour into an unbaked pie shell. Bake at 400° for 10 minutes, then reduce heat to 325° and bake for 45 minutes or until the center of pie is firm and top golden.
Chill before serving.

DEE'S BAKED ALASKA

1 baked 10" pie shell, cooled
3 Tbsp. cornstarch
3 Tbsp. Chocolate-Raspberry liqueur
1½ cups Hershey's chocolate syrup
½ gallon vanilla ice cream
4 egg whites
¼ tsp. cream of tartar
¼ tsp. salt
½ cup sugar
½ tsp. almond flavoring

Optional:
Chopped cherries
Chopped nuts

Combine cornstarch and liqueur in saucepan; stir in chocolate syrup. Cook, stirring constantly, until mixture thickens and bubbles 3 minutes. Remove from heat and cool COMPLETELY. ★Drizzle several spoonfuls of sauce into bottom of pie shell. Scoop ice cream with a large serving spoon - make a layer over sauce, drizzle more sauce and nuts and/or cherries, if desired. Continue layers ending with ice cream. Smooth ice cream, making a higher mound in the center. Freeze while making meringue.

Beat egg whites with cream of tartar and salt until foamy and double in volume. Beat in sugar, gradually, until meringue forms stiff peaks. Add almond flavoring. Frost ice cream with meringue, sealing to pastry edge. Make swirls. Freeze until serving time. Bake at 475° for 3 minutes or until meringue is touched with brown.

Heat remaining sauce. Cut into wedges, drizzle with sauce and serve.

★ You usually have sauce left - if not, it only takes a minute to make more.

This is very easy and quick and can be made several days ahead of time and kept in freezer. Everyone, all ages, loves it!

PECAN DELIGHT PIE

3 egg whites
1 cup sugar
½ tsp. baking powder
1 tsp. vanilla
1 cup chopped pecans
20 Ritz crackers, crushed fine

Beat egg whites until stiff. Beat in sugar, baking powder and vanilla until stiff peaks form. Fold in pecans and cracker crumbs. Pour into a greased 9" glass pie plate. Bake at 350° for 30 minutes.

Good served with whipped cream.

SHERI'S EGGNOG PIE

Pecan crust (recipe follows)
1 envelope unflavored gelatin
¼ cup cold water
4 eggs, separated
1 cup sugar
½ cup milk, scalded
¼ tsp. salt
1 cup whipping cream
3 Tbsp. powdered sugar
¼ tsp. nutmeg

Sprinkle gelatin over water to soften for 5 minutes. In a small bowl, beat egg yolks with ½ cup sugar until light and frothy; pour in scalded milk in a fine stream while beating constantly. Transfer mixture to a heavy saucepan; cook over low heat, stirring constantly, until thick. Do not boil. Remove from heat and stir in gelatin. Pour custard through a sieve into a bowl and cool until thick. Add nutmeg. In a small bowl, beat the egg whites with salt until they hold stiff peaks and gradually beat in ½ cup sugar; fold into custard lightly but thoroughly. Pour into pecan crust. Beat cream with powdered sugar and spoon over pie filling. Sprinkle with nutmeg. Refrigerate at least 6 hours before serving.

Well worth the trouble!
Sheri always used this as the finale at her Christmas party. It was one of the reasons Ed agreed to go caroling.

PECAN CRUST

2 cups shelled pecans
⅓ cup sugar
3 Tbsp. melted butter

In food processor, pulverize nuts; add sugar and melted butter, blend well. Press mixture evenly against bottom and sides of a 10" pie plate. Refrigerate 30 minutes.
Bake at 350° for 12-15 minutes. Cool before filling.

GRASSHOPPER PIE

18 Oreo cookies, crushed
4 Tbsp. melted butter
24 large marshmallows
⅔ cup hot milk
1½ jiggers Creme de Menthe
1 jigger Creme de Cocoa
1 cup whipping cream, whipped

Mix cookie crumbs (processor or blender good for making crumbs) and butter. Reserve 1 tablespoon of crumbs for top. Press crumbs into 9" pie pan and chill.
Dissolve marshmallows in milk. Chill well! Fold into marshmallow mixture the Creme de Menthe and Creme de Cocoa. Fold in whipped cream. Pour into pie shell, sprinkle with tablespoon of crumbs and put in refrigerator for at least 8 hours.

This is so-o-o easy and so-o-o good!
My daughter, Cindy, loves this.

HEAVENLY PUMPKIN PIE

1 Tbsp. unflavored gelatin
¼ cup water
1¼ cups cooked, mashed
  pumpkin
¾ cup milk
2 eggs, separated
1 cup sugar
1 tsp. pumpkin pie spice
1 envelope Dream Whip
Baked pie shell

Soften gelatin in water. Cook pumpkin, egg yolks, ½ cup sugar, milk and spice for 10 minutes. Stir in gelatin mixture and cool. Prepare Dream Whip as directed on package. Beat egg whites, add remaining ½ cup sugar. Fold into pumpkin mixture along with Dream Whip and pour into baked pie shell. Chill.

This recipe comes from a dear friend in Corpus Christi. Ginny is another excellent cook.
Ginny's mother lives with her and between the two of them, there's always something cooking!

SCROGGIN'S BROWN SUGAR PIE

3 cups brown sugar
2 Tbsp. flour
3 eggs
1 cup milk
1 tsp. vanilla
1 cup pecans (optional)
Unbaked pie shell

Beat eggs well, mix with remaining ingredients. Pour into unbaked pie shell. Bake at 325° for 35-40 minutes.

This recipe comes from my grandmother. She always had yummy things in the kitchen when I was growing up. This is just one.

Desserts Cookies & Candy

ANNIE'S LEMON BARS

Crust:
2 cups flour
1 cup margarine
½ cup powdered sugar

Custard:
4 eggs
2 cups sugar
1 tsp. baking powder
3 Tbsp. flour
Juice and rind of 2 lemons

Mix together flour, margarine and powdered sugar. Pat in the bottom of a 9x13 pan. Bake at 350° for 20 minutes.
Beat eggs; add sugar, baking powder and flour. Add lemon juice and rind. Pour over crust and bake at 350° for 20-25 minutes until custard is firm. While still hot, sprinkle with additional powdered sugar. Cool. Cut into bars.

LORETA'S BROWNIES

⅔ cup flour
¼ tsp. salt
2 squares chocolate
1 cup sugar
½ tsp. baking powder
½ cup margarine
2 eggs
1 tsp. vanilla
½ cup chopped pecans

Mix flour with baking powder and salt. Melt butter with chocolate over hot water. Beat eggs well; gradually add sugar, beating well. Beat in chocolate mixture. Mix in flour. Add nuts and vanilla. Bake in a greased 8x8x2 pan at 350° for 25 minutes. Do not overbake. Cool in pan, then cut in squares.

GOOEY BUTTER BARS

1 box yellow cake mix
1 egg, beaten
1 Tbsp. vanilla
1 stick margarine, melted
1 cup finely chopped pecans
2 beaten eggs
8 oz cream cheese
1 box powdered sugar

Combine cake mix, egg, vanilla, margarine and pecans. Spread on the bottom of a 9x13 pan. Beat together eggs, cream cheese and sugar. Pour over crust. Bake at 350° for 30-40 minutes. Center will settle. Do not overbake. Cut into bars.

SPECIAL APPLE SQUARES

1½ cups flour
1½ cups graham cracker crumbs
1 cup packed brown sugar
½ tsp. soda
¾ cup soft butter
1 tsp. cinnamon
1½ cups grated cheddar or American cheese
2½ cups peeled, sliced cooking apples
1 cup sugar
2 tsp. cinnamon
½ cup chopped nuts
Whipped cream

Combine flour, graham cracker crumbs, brown sugar, soda, 1 teaspoon cinnamon and butter until crumbly. Reserve ½ cup crumbs. Pat remaining crumbs into a greased 9x13 pan. Sprinkle cheese on top. Combine apples with sugar and 2 teaspoons cinnamon; sprinkle over cheese. Mix reserved crumbs with nuts and sprinkle on top. Bake at 350° for 35-40 minutes until golden brown. Serve warm with whipped cream. Store in refrigerator.
Serves 12-15.

PECAN BARS

Butter cake mix (yellow)
½ cup melted margarine
4 eggs
½ cup brown sugar
1½ cups dark Karo
1 tsp. vanilla
3 cups chopped pecans

Mix together cake mix (reserve ⅔ cup), melted margarine and one egg. Mixture will be sticky. Grease and flour a 9x13 pan and pat mixture into pan. Bake at 350° for 15 minutes or until golden brown.
With mixer, beat ⅔ cup cake mix, brown sugar, Karo, vanilla and 3 eggs. Pour on top of crust. Cover with chopped pecans. Bake 30-35 minutes. Cool - cut in bars.

Very rich - but very good!

FROSTED DATE BALLS

1¼ cups flour (sift)
¼ tsp. salt
⅓ cup sifted powdered sugar
½ cup margarine
1 Tbsp. milk
1 tsp. vanilla
⅔ cup chopped dates
½ cup chopped pecans

Combine flour and salt; sift together. Cream margarine; add sugar, milk and vanilla. Add flour and salt. Stir in dates and nuts. Roll in one inch balls and place on lightly greased cookie sheet. Bake at 300° for 20 minutes. Roll in powdered sugar.
Makes 3-4 dozen.

This is another of Mother's holiday treats.

DEBBIE'S DEVIL DOGS

6 Tbsp. shortening
1 cup sugar
1 egg
1 cup milk
1 tsp. vanilla
1¼ tsp. soda
¼ tsp. salt
1 tsp. baking powder
2 cups flour
5 Tbsp. cocoa

Frosting:
¾ cup margarine
¾ cup powdered sugar
6 Tbsp. marshmallow creme
1 tsp. vanilla

Cream sugar and shortening, add egg. Add sifted dry ingredients alternately with milk. Drop by teaspoonfuls on greased cookie sheet. Bake at 375° for 7-15 minutes.
Combine frosting ingredients and beat until smooth. Fill between 2 cookies.
Makes about 18

OATMEAL DROP COOKIES

1 cup butter
2 cups brown sugar
2 eggs
¾ cup milk
2½ cups flour
1 tsp. soda
½ tsp. salt
1½ tsp. cinnamon
3 cups rolled oats
½ cup chopped nuts
½ cup raisins

Cream butter; add sugar and mix well. Add eggs; beat thoroughly. Mix soda, salt and cinnamon with flour; add to first mixture alternately with milk. Fold in oats, nuts and raisins. Drop from spoon onto a greased baking sheet. Bake at 400° for 10 minutes.
Makes approx. 100.

OATMEAL CRISPS

½ cup margarine
½ cup brown sugar
½ cup sugar
1 egg
1 cup flour
1 tsp. soda
½ tsp. salt
1 cup oatmeal
1 cup Rice Krispies
1 cup coconut
1 tsp. vanilla

Beat margarine and sugars. Add egg - beat well. Stir in remaining ingredients. Roll in 1" balls on greased cookie sheet. Bake at 350° for 8-10 minutes.
Makes 3-4 dozen.

HERSHEY KISS COOKIES

½ cup margarine
½ cup peanut butter
½ cup sugar
1¾ cups flour
1 tsp. soda
½ tsp. salt
½ cup brown sugar
1 egg
1 tsp. vanilla
Hershey's Kisses

Cream together margarine, peanut butter and sugar. Add flour, soda, salt, brown sugar, egg and vanilla. Roll into 1" balls and dip in granulated sugar. Place on ungreased cookie sheet and slightly flatten. Bake at 325° for 8 minutes. Remove and put Hershey Kiss in center. Cook 2 minutes more.
Makes 3-4 dozen.

The best of 2 flavors!

PEANUT BUTTER CHIPPERS

½ cup butter
⅓ cup sugar
⅓ cup brown sugar
½ tsp. vanilla
1 egg
1¼ cups flour
½ tsp. salt
½ tsp. soda
½ cup crunchy peanut butter
1 cup quick oats
6 oz chocolate chips

Cream butter and sugar, stir in egg and vanilla. Sift flour, salt and soda together, add to creamed mixture along with remaining ingredients. Drop by spoonfuls on greased cookie sheet. Bake at 350° for 10-12 minutes.
Makes 4 dozen.

NO BAKE CHOCOLATE DROPS

2 cups sugar
6 Tbsp. cocoa
1 stick margarine
½ cup milk
3 cups quick oats
¾ cup peanut butter
1 Tbsp. vanilla
1 cup chopped pecans

Combine sugar, cocoa, margarine and milk. Cook over medium heat for 3 minutes. Remove from heat and add oats, peanut butter and vanilla. Fold in nuts. Drop by teaspoonfuls on wax paper. Let set 1-2 hours.

Kids love these!

MOTHER'S FRUITCAKE COOKIES

6 cups chopped nuts
1 lb. chopped dates
1 lb. chopped candied cherries
1 lb. chopped candied
  pineapple
¾ cup flour
1 stick butter
1 cup brown sugar
4 eggs
2¼ cups flour
3 tsp. soda
1 tsp. cinnamon
1 tsp. nutmeg
1 tsp. ground cloves
1 tsp. salt
3 Tbsp. milk
½ cup bourbon

Place chopped nuts and fruits in large bowl. Stir in ¾ cup flour to coat all pieces. Set aside. Cream butter and brown sugar until smooth. Add eggs one at a time, beating well after each addition. Sift together flour, soda, spices and salt; add to creamed mixture. Add milk and bourbon; stir well. Stir in fruit and nuts. Drop by teaspoons onto greased cookie sheet. Bake at 325° for 10 minutes.

People who aren't fond of fruitcake love these. All my relatives look forward to the holiday season, waiting for Mother to start her baking.

MICROWAVE PEANUT BRITTLE

1 cup raw peanuts
1 cup sugar
¼ cup white Karo syrup
¼ cup dark Karo syrup
⅛ tsp. salt
1 tsp. margarine
1 tsp. vanilla
1 tsp. baking soda

Stir together peanuts, sugar, syrup and salt in 1½ qt. casserole. Place in microwave and cook 7-8 minutes on high; stir well after 4 minutes. Remove, add butter and vanilla, blending well. Return to microwave and cook 1-2 minutes more. Syrup will be very hot. Remove and add baking soda. Gently stir until foamy. Pour onto a lightly greased cookie sheet. Cool 1 hour. Break into small pieces.

Great to give at Christmas in decorated tins!

CHOCOLATE CARAMEL CANDY

2 cups flour
1 cup firmly packed brown
  sugar
½ cup soft butter
1 cup chopped pecans
1 cup butter
¾ cup brown sugar
1 cup milk chocolate chips

Combine flour, 1 cup brown sugar and ½ cup soft butter. Mix well and pat into an ungreased 9x13 pan. Sprinkle pecans on top.

Combine 1 cup butter and ¾ cup brown sugar in saucepan. Cook over medium heat, stirring until surface boils. Boil 1 minute, stirring. Pour over crust and pecans. Bake at 350° for 18-20 minutes.

Remove from oven and immediately sprinkle with chocolate chips. Swirl with a knife. Cool and cut into small squares.

PEANUT BUTTER CANDY

1 cup white Karo syrup
1 cup peanut butter
1 cup sugar
5 cups cornflakes

Bring syrup, peanut butter and sugar to a boil. Remove from heat and add cornflakes.

Drop on wax paper and cool. (Be careful not to scorch syrup mixture). You can also do this in the microwave, if desired.

Delicious candy with nutritional value as well.

PEANUT BUTTER BALLS

1 lb. margarine
18 oz jar creamy peanut
  butter
2-3 lbs. powdered sugar
12 oz pkg. chocolate chips
½ slab parafin

Work the margarine, peanut butter and sugar together. Use as much sugar as it takes to be able to roll mixture into small balls.

Melt chocolate and parafin together in top of double boiler. Using a toothpick, dip peanut butter balls in chocolate mixture. Dry on wax paper.

POTATO CANDY

1 small peeled potato
1 box powdered sugar
Smooth peanut butter

Boil potato and drain. Mash with a fork and add powdered sugar. Mixture will be thick. Flour a board with powdered sugar and roll as a pie crust. Spread with peanut butter and roll up as a jelly roll. With a sharp knife, slice into ¼" pieces. Serve.

Very good - no one will believe it's a potato! Doug's very favorite holiday treat.

PRALINES

2 cups sugar
½ tsp. soda
⅔ cup buttermilk
1-2 cup(s) pecans
½ tsp. vanilla

Cook sugar, soda and buttermilk slowly (#3 on electric burner), stirring constantly, to soft ball stage. Remove from heat - add pecans and vanilla. Beat until mixture loses gloss (it will look creamy). Takes about 5-7 minutes of beating. Drop by tablespoons on waxed paper to cool. Makes 2½-3 dozen.

STRAWBERRY PIZZA

Crust:
1 cup flour
¼ cup powdered sugar
1 stick margarine

Filling:
8 oz cream cheese
½ tsp. vanilla
½ cup sugar
¼ tsp. lemon juice

Topping:
1 cup mashed strawberries
4 Tbsp. sugar
1 Tbsp. cornstarch
½ tsp. red food coloring

1 qt. sliced strawberries

Combine crust ingredients and pat into a pizza pan. Bake at 325° for 15 minutes. Cool.
Beat together filling ingredients. Spread over cooled crust.
Combine topping ingredients and cook over medium heat until thickened. Cool. Spread over cheese filling. Cover with the sliced strawberries. Cover and refrigerate at least 2 hours. Cut in wedges as you would a pizza.

This is so different and a lot of "fun" to serve.

FRUIT PIZZA

1 (18 oz) roll slice and bake
  sugar cookies
8 oz softened cream cheese
4½ oz Cool Whip
1 pt. fresh strawberries, halved
2-3 sliced bananas, (dip in
  lemon juice)
1 lb. can cling peaches, drained
8 oz can pineapple chunks,
  drained

Spread dough in pizza pan. Bake at 350° for 10-12 minutes.
Blend cream cheese and Cool Whip. Spread over cooled crust. Arrange strawberries around outside edge, bananas next, then peaches and pineapple in center. Garnish with whole strawberries if desired.
May also top with orange sauce. Recipe follows.

ORANGE SAUCE

½ cup sugar
Dash salt
1 Tbsp. cornstarch
½ cup orange juice
2 Tbsp. lemon juice
¼ cup water
½ tsp. grated orange peel

Stir together sugar, salt and cornstarch. Gradually, stir in orange juice, lemon juice and water. Cook over medium heat, stirring until mixture thickens and boils. Boil one minute. Remove from heat and stir in peel. Cool.

A refreshing summer dessert! It's good with or without the sauce.

PUMPKIN DESSERT

3 eggs
1 can pumpkin
1 cup sugar
13 oz can evaporated milk
1 spice cake mix
1½ sticks margarine
½ cup chopped pecans

Beat eggs; add pumpkin, sugar and evaporated milk. Blend well and pour into a 9x13 pan. Sprinkle cake mix (dry) on top. Melt margarine and pour over cake mix. Sprinkle with pecans. Bake at 350° for 45-60 minutes or until a knife inserted in center comes out clean.
Serve with whipped cream.

PISTACHIO DESSERT

53 Ritz crackers, crushed
1¼ sticks margarine, melted
1 qt. softened vanilla ice cream
1½ cups milk
2 pkgs. instant Pistachio pudding
8 oz Cool Whip
Optional: grated pistachio nuts

Mix cracker crumbs and margarine. Pat into a 9x13 pan. Combine ice cream, milk and pudding mix with electric mixer, beating well. Pour over crust. Refrigerate at least 3 hours. Cover with Cool Whip and sprinkle with nuts, if desired. Refrigerate at least 2 more hours.

DEVIL'S FOOD QUICKIE

½ cup cocoa
1 cup brown sugar, sifted
2 cups water
1 (6¼ oz) pkg. miniature marshmallows
1 pkg. Devil's Food cake mix
1½ tsp. vanilla
1 cup coarsely chopped toasted pecans

Mix cocoa, sugar and water in a 9x13 pan. Sprinkle with marshmallows. Prepare cake mix according to directions, but adding vanilla to batter. Spoon batter over mixture in pan. Top with nuts. Bake at 350° for 50 minutes. Allow to cool slightly, then cut in serving size pieces and serve sauce side up.

I use a very large cooking spoon and serve it up like cobbler in small bowls. Make sure you flip it over so sauce is on top.

This cake gets raves!

UNCLE MAC'S COBBLER

1 stick margarine
1 cup flour
1 cup sugar
Pinch of salt
1 tsp. baking powder
⅔ cup milk
1 (#303) can peaches, drained
2 cups or 1 can water-packed cherries, drained

Melt margarine in 8" or 9" square pan. Mix flour, sugar, salt, baking powder and milk for batter. Spoon over melted margarine. Top with fruit. Bake at 325° for 1 hour. The dough rises and covers fruit with a crust as it bakes.

BANANA PUDDING I

¼ cup cornstarch
1 cup sugar
Pinch salt
4 cups milk, divided
3 egg yolks
2 Tbsp. butter
1 box vanilla wafers
4-6 large bananas, sliced
1½ tsp. vanilla

Meringue:
3 egg whites
¼ tsp. cream of tartar
½ tsp. vanilla
6 Tbsp. sugar

Mix cornstarch, sugar, salt and 2 cups milk. Cook until thick before adding egg yolks. Beat egg yolks and add a little to hot mixture - then add to pot. Put back on burner and cook 5 minutes. Add butter. Let cool while lining pan (9x13) with wafers and bananas.

Add remaining 2 cups milk to pudding along with 1½ teaspoons. vanilla. You want the pudding fairly thin - it will thicken as it cools. Pour over bananas. Top with meringue. Bake at 450° until meringue is golden brown.

Meringue:
Beat egg whites and cream of tartar until soft peaks form; add vanilla and add sugar, gradually, beating until stiff peaks form.

This pudding is well worth the effort!

BANANA PUDDING II

Large jello instant vanilla pudding
3 cups milk
1 can condensed milk
8 oz Cool Whip
1 tsp. vanilla
4-6 bananas
Small box vanilla wafers

Beat pudding, milk, condensed milk and vanilla until smooth. Stir in Cool Whip. Layer bananas, vanilla wafers and pudding. Chill.

This is very good and rich with absolutely no effort!

BAKED CUSTARD

4 slightly beaten eggs
½ cup sugar
¼ tsp. salt
2½ cups milk, scalded
1 tsp. vanilla
¼ tsp. almond flavoring
Freshly grated nutmeg
★ Brown sugar

Combine eggs, sugar and salt. Slowly stir in milk and flavorings. Set custard cups in pan. Fill pan with 1" of water. Pour custard into cups. Sprinkle nutmeg on top. Bake at 325° for 45 minutes. Serve warm or chilled.
Serves 8 (5 oz servings).

★ If desired, put 1 teaspoon brown sugar in cup before pouring custard in.

SHELLEY'S BROWNIE CUP CAKES

1 box Supreme brownie mix -
  family size
⅔ cup water
2 eggs
8 oz cream cheese
½ cup sugar
⅛ tsp. salt
6 oz semi-sweet chocolate
  chips

Line muffin tins with paper liners.
Blend brownie mix, water, eggs and syrup (in mix). Fill muffin cups ⅔ full.
Combine cream cheese, sugar and salt. Beat on low one minute. Add chips.
Drop 1 tablespoon of filling into each muffin cup. Bake at 350° for 20-25 minutes.
Store in the refrigerator.

One of the many treats Shelley introduced me to. She never comes for a visit unless she brings some luscious treat. She's a wonderful friend who truly loves to entertain and cook.

PRALINE SAUCE

1 cup brown sugar
¼ cup light Karo syrup
½ cup half and half
2 Tbsp. butter
1 tsp. vanilla
⅛ tsp. salt
1 cup pecans (or more)

Combine all ingredients. Cook over medium heat, stirring, for about 10 minutes or until thick and smooth. Cool slightly. Serve over ice cream or pound cake.

Very addictive!

RICH VANILLA ICE CREAM

4 eggs
2½ cups sugar
5 cups milk
2 cups whipping cream
2 cups half and half
4½ tsp. vanilla
½ tsp. salt

Beat eggs 3 minutes. Gradually add sugar and continue beating until stiff. Add cream, half and half, vanilla and salt. Beat well. Gradually add milk and mix thoroughly. Freeze in ice cream maker.

CREAM CHEESE BROWNIES

2 pkgs. (4 oz each) Baker's
 German sweet chocolate
10 Tbsp. butter, divided
1 (8 oz) pkg. cream cheese
½ cup sugar
2 eggs
2 Tbsp. flour
1 tsp. vanilla
4 eggs
1½ cups sugar
1 tsp. baking powder
½ tsp. salt
1 cup flour
1 cup chopped, toasted pecans
1 Tbsp. vanilla
1 tsp. almond flavoring

Melt chocolate and 6 tablespoons butter over low heat, stirring constantly. Cool. Blend remaining butter with cream cheese until softened. Gradually add ½ cup sugar, beating well. Blend in 2 eggs, 2 tablespoons flour and 1 teaspoon vanilla. Set aside.

Beat 4 eggs until thick. Gradually add 1½ cups sugar, beating well. Add baking powder, salt and 1 cup flour. Blend in chocolate mixture, pecans, 1 tablespoon vanilla and almond flavoring.

Spread half of chocolate batter in greased 9x13 pan, add cheese mixture, spreading evenly. Top with tablespoons of remaining chocolate mixture. Take a spatula and swirl through batter to marble. Bake at 350° for 35-40 minutes or until a toothpick comes out clean. Cool. Cut into squares.

I cover with foil after 20 minutes. Leave until cool. Brownies are more moist.

JONI'S HIP HUGGERS

14 oz pkg. caramels
⅔ cup evaporated milk
1 pkg. German chocolate cake
 mix
¾ cup melted margarine
1 cup chopped pecans
1 cup semi-sweet chocolate
 chips

Cook caramels and ⅓ cup milk in large saucepan over low heat, stirring until melted. Set aside. Combine cake mix, margarine, remaining milk and nuts. Stir by hand until mixture holds together.

Press half of dough into a greased 9x13 pan. Bake 6 minutes at 350°. Remove from oven and sprinkle with chocolate chips. Spread caramel mixture over chips. Crumble and press remaining dough over top. Return to oven and bake 15-18 minutes. Cool slightly. Refrigerate 30 minutes to set caramel.
Makes 48.

Joni stays so busy, I don't know when she finds the time to make all her delicious desserts.

INDEX

COOKIES, CANDIES
& DESSERTS

COOKIES

CANDIES

DESSERTS

Notes

Notes

Notes

Notes

Reorder Additional Copies